SHAMAN

Examines the background and characteristics of classical
shamanism, as still practised today, and looks at the way in
which primitive shamanism has developed throughout history.

SHAMANISM
The Foundations of Magic

by

Ward Rutherford

THE AQUARIAN PRESS
Wellingborough, Northamptonshire

First published 1986

British Library Cataloguing in Publication Data

Rutherford, Ward
   Shamanism: the foundations of magic
   1. Shamanism
   I. Title
   291.6′2   BL2370.S5

ISBN 0-85030-453-9

*The Aquarian Press is part of the
Thorsons Publishing Group*

Printed and bound in Great Britain

Contents

Acknowledgements

The author would like to acknowledge the generous assistance given to him in the preparation of this book by Michael and Sandra Harner, by Dr James Lovelock whose *Gaia: A New Look at Life on Earth* places on a scientific foundation what shamanism has been saying throughout its infinitely long history. To Marjorie Durward, Mrs C. P. Raafat, Bernard Rutherford, Dr Celia Green of the Institute of Psychophysical Research at Oxford, Dr Susan Blackmore of the Brain and Perception Unit at Bristol University and, especially, Jennifer Chambers for their informed and helpful views on the psychology of shamanism.

PART I: THE SETTING

1. Origins and Definitions

They are nomads, moving with the herds up to the grassy mountain slopes in summer, down to the sheltered lowlands in winter, an entire community, striking the tepi-like tents they call *yurts* to re-erect them on their new pastures.

It is night and the yurts are black cones against the sky, the tops of the frame-poles sticking out through the smokeholes like bean-stakes. All, save one, are in darkness. Much larger than the rest, its covering of stitched hides decorated with symbols, it glows like a lantern from the fire blazing inside.

Toward it, men, women, children, even babes carried in bundles on their mother's backs, are converging like ants on honey. Except for the prattle of the very youngest, they walk silently, as if the occasion is too serious for idle chatter.

Ethnically they are Mongols, members of that ancient root-race whose descendants inhabit all the surrounding lands, south eastern Siberia, Tibet, migrating outward as far as Korea and Japan, leaving their traits upon the Eskimo and the American Indians, founders of the pre-Columbian civilizations. They may even have been the forefathers of one of the most gifted races the earth has ever seen, the Sumerians.

One behind another, the little family groups slip through the tent-flap. Within, decorations much like those on the outside cover the walls, the fire's flickering light giving them life. Somewhere a flautist plays a soft, plaintive melody.

Stewards usher each group to benches arranged in a horseshoe, leaving free an open aisle and an area round the fire, raked and swept clean.

The only object placed in this area is an oval, flat, skin drum, also embellished with figures, propped against a straight tree trunk stripped of bark, its top protruding up through the smokehole. The assembling groups know the care with which it has been chosen. Among all the trees of the forest, this alone is an offshoot of the Great Tree that stands at the centre of the earth.

Whenever the fire shows any sign of dying down, the stewards pile on more wood. At other times one of them tosses on to it handfuls of powder from a pouch at his waist and the flames lick up blue, green, red, or the smoke which fills the hot, human-smelling interior, forming a cloud above the heads of the assembly as it tries to escape, becomes fragrant and heady.

From time to time, the stewards glance covertly, to see if all are yet gathered. Even when they have assured themselves they are, for a long period, so long that the children grow restive, nothing happens. The hum of conversation grows louder; then, suddenly dies on gasps of expectancy.

The tent flap opens. On the threshold stands an extraordinary figure, dressed in an ankle-length robe, masked, and wearing an elaborate headdress among whose constituent elements a span of horns and the wings and head of a bird can be made out. He holds a staff, ribbons and multi-coloured strings dangling from it.

He is the tribal shaman.

For several moments, like the actor he truly is, he stands motionless as though determined to make the most impressive entrance possible. Then, oblivious of the shrieks of the terrified children, bones and glittering metal ornaments sewn on to his cloak jingling and rattling, sweeping his staff before him so that strings and ribbons fly, he strides down the aisle. As he passes, more coloured ribbons sewn at the collar and down the back of his robe flutter behind him.

He makes for the cleared area round the fire, grasps his staff in both fists and jabs it into the ground, then takes up the drum and, at first scarcely more than caressing it, whispering as he does so, seems to seek a rhythm with which to accompany the flute-player's plangent melody.

Minutes pass. Very slowly tempo and volume of the drumming increase. Imperceptibly, the roles of flute and drum are reversed, the flute-player providing the accompaniment to the complex rhythm-pattern of the drummer.

And the shaman's whisper has converted itself into a song, a luring call to the spirits. Though improvized for the occasion, its melody and choruses are familiar to the gathering who, aware that they are present not as passive spectators but as participants in a spiritual enterprise, join in the words.

The song seems unending and, as the singer gets caught up in it and in the rhythm of his own drumming, he begins a slow shuffling dance. Clapping, stamping their feet to the beat, his audience encourage him.

All the time the pace of the drumming and accompanying dance increases. It is as if the drum had acquired a life and a momentum of its own to which the shaman is slave. Soon, he is moving with such speed, whirling, spinning, leaping, that he seems one with the firelight, the metal and bone adornments of his costume flashing, the ribbons down his back writhing.

Momentary pauses lead the spectators to anticipate a climax. But in that selfsame moment he will have begun again, throwing himself with greater abandon into song, dance, drumming.

Again and again the caesura; the held breath of the spectators; and again and again he flings himself back into the dance.

Then, at last, long after any of the watchers had believed possible, he drops to his knees, drum falling from his hands, to be caught by his assistants as it rolls like a hoop.

The shaman himself lies prone on the ground, a corpse, and truly a corpse, for his soul has left its bodily home. It is climbing the tree trunk, one with the rising smoke, seeking a way through the smokehole, travelling to the spirit world . . .

The Shaman in History

Foreign and bizarre as the scene may appear to us it still has familiar elements. One thinks immediately of a concert by a jazz soloist, the gradual building up of a rapport between performer and audience in which they seem to merge into one greater entity. Or of the congregation in church, chapel, synagogue or mosque. The music. The celebrant, the mediator with the Other World, garbed in the vestments of his office.

That these familiar elements should be present is hardly surprising. Decorations remarkably similar to those on the walls of the Siberian shaman's yurts are to be found in the paleolithic caves of Southern France, Spain and North Africa. Among the figures in these teeming scenes is the famous 'Sorcerer of Les Trois Frères', his costume corresponding in every detail with that of the shaman. By Joseph Campbell's computation at least fifty-five such figures have been made out in the various caves.

Yet even then shamanism was old. It probably began much earlier in the hunter-gatherer phase, one that has occupied by far the greater proportion of our evolutionary past. Indeed, if the period from the emergence of the first recognizable humanoids to the present day is assumed to be a hundred years, then our present, post-hunter phase, would represent a mere three minutes.

During that immensely long period shamanism has exerted its influence. Some of the ways it has done so will emerge in the course of this book. But it was at work long before Islam, Christianity, Judaism, Buddhism or even Hinduism saw the light of day. The religion of the ancient Mesopotamian civilizations, Chinese Taoism, and possibly the oldest of all, Persian Zoroastrianism – from whose priesthood, the Magi, we get the word 'magic' – all bear its imprint.

In Celtic myth, we are told how the great Irish Druid, Mag Roth, having donned his bull's skin cloak and his bird headdress, rose up with the smoke to ascend to the sky. The Scythians, neighbours of the Celts in their original Danubian homelands, and the shapers of so much that came to be regarded as Celtic had their Enarees, shamans in all but name.

Among the honorifics of the Norse Odin was 'the Great Shaman' and that it was no empty title is shown by the myth of his acquisition of the magical runes.

Though shamanism had vanished from the religion of the Greeks long before they are known to history, many of their gods still show the marks of their ancestry. Even the chief of them, Zeus, is not past taking on the forms of swan and bull, two of the most shamanistic creatures, when he consorts with mortal women.

It left other marks on Greek culture. Recalling that the drama was in origin a sacred rite dedicated to Dionysus, the circular area of the amphitheatre where the chorus performed – the *orchestra* – must have been the descendant and counterpart of that zone before the shaman's fire where his drama was enacted, especially when we realize that at the centre of the Greek amphitheatre there stood an altar on which a fire was kept burning throughout the performance.* And, as the works of A. T. Hatto and of A. Lommel show, it is not only drama, but all the arts which owe their inception to the shaman.

Even among the Romans, whose religion was of a severely

---

* There is a linguistic link between *mimesis*, the actor's impersonation of a character, and the actual taking over of his personality by it. Hence in the early drama the principal actor did not impersonate the deity; he actually became Dionysus.

practical kind in which veneration or sacrifice was accorded strictly in the hope of return, the *flamen dialis* betrays his forebears.

Not only does the shaman cast his giant's shadow down history, he recurs through it with the regularity of the proverbial bad penny. In classical Greece, in latter-day Rome, in the early Renaissance, and especially in our own times.

Nor is he subject to spatial limitations. Spin a globe and prod a finger at any point in it and you can be certain that in some way, at some time, he dwelt there. He is to be found from the Arctic to the Australian outback. He was as familiar to Polynesian islanders as to many of the peoples living on the great landmass of Africa.

What is the Shaman?

Yet what exactly is the shaman?

He proves extremely elusive to define. Or, one might say, ten writers on the subject will each define him differently.

He is certainly not the propagator of a system of doctrines. He does not apportion blame, but, like a doctor in his treatment of disease, responds to a particular crisis whether individual or communal with a remedy designed to meet it and it alone. The sufferers and the cause of suffering are alike blameless, just as to the doctor the virus is neutral.

At the same time, he does not share in a single body of universal knowledge. In this he obviously differs from the Western doctor, who regardless of nationality will have available to him the same training, drugs and procedures.

As to the word 'shaman' itself, that it comes from the language of the Tungus people of eastern Siberia is generally agreed. Some believe it is cognate with the Sanskrit *sramana*, an ascetic, while for others it means 'one who is excited or moved'.

The late Professor Vilmos Dioszegi, writing in the fifteenth edition of *Encyclopedia Britannica*, finds its derivation in the Tunguso-Manchurian word *saman*, formed from the verb *sa-*. This implies a relationship with the Indo-European root yielding the French *savoir* and the Spanish *saber*, both meaning 'to know'. In this way the shaman becomes 'he who knows', giving the word an etymological relationship to such familiar words as 'witch' and 'wizard', both from an Indo-European root meaning 'to see' or 'to know', and present in the forms of the French *voir*, the Latin *videre*, to see, and the German *wissen*, to know.

This knowledge does not take us far in trying to identify the shaman. So, if etymology fails, what of the usage of the word? At once we are plunged into controversy. For some it has become a portmanteau into which to load all mediators with the supernatural, the African Juju-man, the Caribbean *Obeah*, the Voodoo priest, the Amerindian medicine-man; others show a discriminating selectivity as to what is and what is not to be regarded as shamanistic.

Thus, at one extreme, to I. M. Lewis, studying him from the standpoint of an anthropologist, the shaman is 'a person of either sex who has mastered spirits and who can at will introduce them into his own body'. At the other, Dioszegi regards shamanism as applying primarily to the north Asian, Ural-Altaic peoples. Many of the manifestations occurring outside this area are, in his view, no more than 'detached traits' and not necessarily of themselves shamanistic at all. For example, though the sorcerers and medicine-men of many cultures claim to communicate with the Other World, unlike the shaman, they may have attained their position by study and the application of codified knowledge.

Foremost among scholars of the subject, Mircea Eliade characterizes the shaman by one unique activity: his soul-journey into the Other World. Campbell takes much the same view.

But the shaman is quite unlike the priest in another respect. For the priest, those with whom he mediates are beings of ineffable, unattainable superiority to mere humans. The shaman admits of no such superiority. The spirits are neither good nor evil. They differ from mortals only in their greater powers. Otherwise, like us, they are self-seeking, amenable to flattery and liable to lose their temper, and when angered often implacably vindictive towards those who have displeased them, even if the act is no more than the inadvertent breaking of an unknown taboo.

Like humans, the spirits do not freely part with what is theirs. Luckily they are also capable of being duped and so to gain his ends or those of his people, the shaman will not scruple to employ deception. He is, in fact, the Great Trickster.

In so far as the concepts of good and evil exist at all in shamanism, they apply not to the spirits but to the nature of the shaman himself. 'Black' or malevolent ones have always been recognized and it is against their machinations that the 'white' or good shaman may be called to use his skills. Often these evil-doers are female, as in Castaneda's *The Teachings of Don Juan*, where the old shaman's greatest enemy is the woman whom he calls the *diablera*, the worker of devilries. As we shall see, gender is not without significance.

The Role of the Shaman

None of the foregoing can be said to give us an entire or satisfactory picture of either the shaman or his calling. So, since he has eluded all our other nets, can we, perhaps, associate him with a particular phase of human social development?

One of religion's greatest historians, Father Wilhelm Schmidt, discusses this in *The Origins of the Idea of God*. For him, the coming of the shaman marks humanity's first systematic attempt to come to terms with the supernatural. Of the many stark mysteries by which humans were surrounded, death must have been one of the most dreadful. What happened in that moment when the living, moving creature became an inert lump? Something had fled: a spark, the spirit – the words are actually related. The problem is admirably developed by an Eskimo shaman talking to the Danish explorer Rasmussen:

> The greatest peril of life lies in the fact that human food consists entirely of souls. All the creatures we have to kill and eat, all those we have to strike down and destroy to make clothes for ourselves, have souls, as we have.*

It was out of their anxiety that, in Father Schmidt's view, men and women were impelled to develop pre- and post-hunt rituals to assist their prey on the journey to the Other World. In a typical example the author describes how, in the early morning, before setting out with the hunt, a pygmy-artist draws a picture of his quarry on the ground. In the evening, having succeeded in the chase, he takes blood and hair from the slaughtered animal and lays them on his picture. The following morning, as the rising sun touches it, he rubs out the whole image.

In similar rites found elsewhere, after its flesh has been eaten, the bones of the animal will be taken to some place which members of its species are known to frequent. There they are carefully laid out in a representation of itself in order that its spirit may, if it chooses, return to take up its abode once more.

Such rituals suffered from an inherent disadvantage. There

---

* Cited in *The Intellectual Culture of the Iglulik Eskimos*, Copenhagen, 1929.

was no way of knowing whether the client-spirit had actually been mollified or was now happily reunited with the spirits of his ancestors. Before this could come about a specialist, someone who could travel to the Other World itself and report back from it, was needed. He was the shaman.

Many scholars have seen in this early phase the beginnings of what has come to be called 'totemism'. As a result of his visits to the Other World, the shaman would gradually forge links of friendship with one or other of the animal spirits who inhabited it. The creature would manifest its own goodwill towards both him and his tribe by granting favours. The recipients would requite these by adopting the creature as their totem, mythologically tracing their own origins back to it, so that it became the common ancestor of the tribe or clan.

While the entire topic of totemism is surrounded by fierce debate, it is certainly true that spirit-animals, often spoken of as 'power animals', play a significant part in shamanism.

To Schmidt, then, the shaman as religion's progenitor, arises out of a particular socio-economic environment, that of peoples who have passed from the most primitive form of hunting and who may be moving towards pastoral-nomadism.

The Crisis of the Shaman
This chapter sets out to discuss origins and definitions. So far as the latter goes we have largely been concerned with what is *not* shamanism.

There is, I believe, one element in Dioszegi's definition which encapsulates the essence. He tells us that though the sorcerers of many cultures claim to communicate with the Other World, unlike the shaman they have attained their position by *deliberate study and the application of rational knowledge*. In other words, the shaman does not acquire his position in this way. It is acquired through vision and trance, and the gift for these comes from a personal crisis. All else springs from that one event.

The nature of the crisis will be examined in Chapter 3, but we can perhaps make one further call on the evidence of the Eskimo quoted previously. He describes how, desiring to become a shaman, he sought an instructor. Wherever he turned, he was refused. Finally, he went alone into the bleak Arctic reaches. In a menacing silence broken only by the wolf-howl of the wind, moods of melancholia alternated with those of manic euphoria.

In the midst of such a fit of mysterious and overwhelming delight I became a shaman, not knowing myself how it came about ... I could see and hear in a totally different way. I had gained my enlightenment, the shaman's light of brain and body, and this in such a manner that it was not only I who could see through the darkness of life, but the same bright light also shone out from me, imperceptible to human beings but visible to all the spirits of earth and sky and sea.

Another witness, this time a young woman of our own age and culture, uses almost the same words. Describing her metamorphosis into a shaman, Dr Leslie Gray told an interviewer from an American magazine, 'The world suddenly seemed less foreign, more familiar; things just seemed to fit together more in every way'.

Of course, this experience is not entirely limited to the shaman. Most of us have probably had some inkling of it as, for instance, when standing alone in some solitary and majestic landscape we may have been overwhelmed by the sense of its living presence, of the interaction of its parts and of our own part in that interaction. It is a sensation tacit in the phrase 'communing with nature' and in what the Romans called the 'spirit of place', the *genius loci*.

It is what Freud designates 'the oceanic feeling', one which, for want of a better description, might be said to be the sensation of being a part of something infinitely greater than oneself.

For most of us, experiences of this kind may be pleasurable, and perhaps even revelatory. In a few cases they may lead to a fundamental change of life, something akin to the famous Enlightenment of the Buddha. More often, they are purely transitory.

However, it is not difficult to imagine how the shaman's rigorous and specialized training can lead to a proportionate increase in its intensity and, by so doing, change its quality. Indeed, such is its intensity that three contemporary western shamans, Dr Michael Harner and Carlos Castaneda and, to some extent, Leslie Gray, are forced to draw a distinction between the appearances most of us know and those perceived by the shaman. Castaneda writes of 'ordinary reality' and 'non-ordinary reality'; Harner, perhaps more precisely, of the 'Ordinary State of Consciousness' (OSC) and the 'Shamanic State of Consciousness'. In it, things shed their outward reality to reveal their inner essence. As Castaneda tells us, what appears to most of us simply as a raven flapping across a wintry sky may, to the shaman, also be an emissary from the Other World and, as such, quite recognizable and distinguishable from the rest of its kind.

For the shaman, the 'inner essence' is *the* reality; all else, illusion. He would agree with Plato in his famous Simile of the Cave. According to this, the run of men and women are like prisoners who have spent their entire lives in a cave. Objective reality is, for them, simply the succession of shadows cast on its walls by the firelight. Very, very occasionally one of them (whom the author likens to the philosopher) manages to make a brief escape, and thereby glimpses true reality. Not only does the image remain with him when he is returned to his gaol, it also affects the way he sees the shadows on the walls for ever more.

And in this we have the core of shamanism: it is a mode of apprehension.

2. The Eternal Conflict

There are two dangers in attempting a definition of shamanism. While Dioszegi is right to admonish caution, a definition that is too restrictive, limiting him, say, to the area where the actual name occurs, will leave us without a classification for phenomena occurring half a world away showing such numerous striking similarities that they cannot be dismissed as mere 'detached traits'. By the same token, one that is cast too wide may lead to the inclusion of what may not, strictly speaking, be shamanistic at all.

As far as the latter goes, we are obviously most likely to be led astray where there are superficial resemblances. Since shamanism is characterized by ecstasy, many scholars have tended to treat every form of ecstasy, particularly in an archaic or primitive environment as, *ipso facto*, shamanistic, ignoring the possibility that it may take more than one form.

Wilhelm Schmidt, as we have seen, regards shamanism as lying near the heart of the idea of God. One of the foundations of his case is the concept of the 'Sky God' which he finds recurrent in shamanistic systems and sees as evolving into the One God of the Judaic, Muslim and Christian religions.

For my part, I believe that a careful reading of the data reveals the existence, not of one, but of two separate roots of religion, only one of which is truly shamanistic. And for the purposes of our present inquiry, it is important we should be able to distinguish them.

If one considers the images of Egyptian gods over the period from the Old Kingdom, that is to say the middle of the Third Millennium BC onwards, something curious emerges. Male deities are depicted in four forms; at first as birds or animals, later as animals with perhaps a hand or arm, then as complete humans but with bird and animal heads; finally, they are fully human. On the other hand, female deities – Isis, Nut, Shu, Sati or Selket – are consistently depicted in human form. In some portrayals, anthropomorphic female and theriomorphic male actually appear side by side.

From Egyptian iconography, a generalized conclusion might seem to be that while it traces the evolution of *gods* from archaic totemic animal to the fully human, no such evolution had occurred among the *goddesses*.

As a matter of fact, this same dichotomy can be found in other places and traced back to well before the period when the Egyptian civilization was at its height. Since, as we have seen, the shaman is associated with the hunting phase, it is appropriate that in the earliest depictions, those of the cave-drawings, he appears in just such a setting.

At Mal'ta, near Lake Baikal, models of flying ducks or geese carved from mammoth ivory have been found, and representations of flying birds are far from rare. Campbell suggests that the swastika, a symbol which occurs in Chinese and Tibetan Buddhism and is associated with the spiritual flight of the Buddha may well have evolved from the image of the flying bird. As flight-metaphors are common in shamanism, one may well suspect that the people who produced the Lake Baikal geese practised it.

Both geese and cave drawings are dated to the Paleolithic, that is to say to the period roughly from 30,000 to 10,000 BC. But broadly contemporaneous with them are those often crudely carved figures somewhat ironically called the 'Venuses', such as those of Laussel, Lespugue and Willendorf. What they portray are women, naked, heavy-breasted, steatopygous, invariably pregnant – but recognizably human.

So here we see two traditions. One is male and represents the supernatural either in terms of those who meditate with it, i.e. the shaman as in the cave drawings, or of the totemic creatures who are the shaman's familiars. The other is female and from its earliest known times has deities in human form.* How did this situation come about?

I believe we have two clues. One clue is provided by Campbell who tells us that among the North American Indian tribes the

---

* There are, of course, exceptions. The human figures found in the caves at Pech Merle near Cahors in southern France have been identified as female, though it has to be said they are so roughly drawn as to be at least ambiguous.

rite of initiation into adulthood took two divergent forms. In one, that of the hunters, the young man was taken by his father to some remote place there to seek communion with the spirits. In the other, that of the agriculturists, the initiation was public and communal.

The other clue is the pregnancy of the Venuses.

The Symbolism of Fire

Hunting must always have been a primarily male activity. Even if they wanted to participate, it was rare for women to be able to do so since they were fully occupied with tasks much like those our society still delegates to them: cleaning, sewing and cooking.

The last involved fire and so connects with the other feminine chore of maintaining the tribal hearth. However, before the discovery of the means of making it were known, fire could be obtained only from naturally occurring – hence 'divine' – sources, spontaneous combustion, lightning strikes and the like.

The rarity and unpredictability of these, made conservation of the fire, once lit, vital. Furthermore, when the tribe moved to new hunting grounds or pastures, it had to be taken with them in some form, perhaps as a piece of glowing touchwood or a brand.

The evidence that women – particularly pre- or post-menstrual ones – were the guardians of the hearth is overwhelming. Fire is repeatedly connected with female deities. Athena, one of the oldest of the Greek goddesses, has an ambiguous relationship with the smith-god Hephaistos, who like the Roman Vulcan is associated with the volcano, which is, of course, another of the naturally occurring sources of fire. For the Romans, the patroness of the hearth was Vesta whose six virgins maintained the perpetual flame in her temple.

Caesar cites Minerva as among the deities most revered by the Celts and, though there are other interpretations, he is generally thought to have been applying a Graeco-Roman name to Brigid, widely venerated throughout the British Isles. Her association with fire is witnessed by the fact that after the conversion of Ireland, a cathedral dedicated to St Brigid, apocryphal mother of the Virgin, was built at one of her main cult centres, that at Kildare. Here a perpetual flame still is maintained by nine nuns and it is no doubt significant that in most churches the sanctuary lamps, relics of the perpetual fire, are tended by women.

One possible meaning of the name Guinevere, that of the wife of King Arthur, is 'the white flame' and the French Celticist

Professor Jean Markale suggests that the story of her abduction
and of her rescue by Lancelot is a fire-theft myth.

On top of this there is anthropological and linguistic data.
The Sanskrit word *yoni* means both a fire-hole and the vagina
and the Chinese word *yin* may have a similar derivation. The
stories which make up the *Satyricon* of Petronius come from a
diversity of sources, some of great antiquity. One records how a
powerful wizard revenged himself on a witch who had rejected
his advances by making a flame come from between her thighs
so that the people of her village were forced to apply to her when
their lamps and fires needed lighting. Other anthropological
evidence connecting women with fire comes from regions as
widely separated as Papua-New Guinea, Australia, Maori New
Zealand, Africa, India, Indonesia, Mexico and Borneo.

The Earth Mother
Since fire symbolizes life, the activity of fire-tending is probably
connected with and symbolic of what was obviously far and away
the most important of all the female functions: that of generating
new life.

Notwithstanding Freud who, in *Totem and Taboo*, regards
ignorance of the male role in conception as the brandmark of the
backward primitive, there is every indication that the discovery
came comparatively late in history. It is one interpretation of the
Greek myth of Apollo's appropriation of the sanctuary of Gaia.

That the Greeks were by no means alone in their biological
ignorance is demonstrated by the persistence in so many
societies, the Celtic among them, of matrilineal succession.
Even in contemporary Judaism, Jewishness is passed on through
the mother not the father.

With her capacity to procreate, apparently unaided, it is easy
to understand the awe the female inspired. Hers was a magic
infinitely more potent than any of which the male was capable.
Even the hunter was indebted to the female of each species for
providing the animals he pursued.

There was another inescapable fact. Like the female, the
earth itself yielded unaided. It was – must be – the Great
Mother.

The pregnant Venuses are far from the only representations
of her. The burial mounds, too, take their form from her, that of
a passage terminating in a dome-shaped chamber, the
representation of vagina and uterus, a fact emphasized by
carvings, portraying the vulva, found on the entrance stones on

many of them. Inside it the corpse is often laid in a bed of conch-shells whose own shape evokes the female genitalia. It was usually disposed in the pre-natal position and daubed with red ochre, representing the blood in which the new born are veiled.

Those comparatively rare locations where the soil is red, usually because of the presence in it of haematite (the name is derived from the Greek word for blood, *haema*), take on a special significance. It is her menstruum. For Taoists, the mineral cinnabar which occurs as a lode of brilliant scarlet, was regarded as of special efficacy in all alchemic operations. Among the Egyptians an amulet of gold, carnelian or red enamelware and called 'the blood of Isis' was hung round the necks of mummies before entombment.

And to the Earth Mother, mortal women were both microcosm and coadjutrix. Hence the mystique which accumulated round the menstrual cycle; hence the anxiety with which men watched for any cessation in the flow.

The power accreting to women as accomplices of the Earth Mother has led some observers to conclude that they must have been the first mediators with the supernatural and, initially, it was they who were responsible for the propitiatory rituals by which the hunter allayed the irate spirits of the creatures he had slain. They were, that is to say, the first shamans. The truth is that everything combines to suggest that shamanism was, if not exclusively, at least predominantly a male calling from earliest times.

Naturally, the picture is often confused. In an area whose history extends back to the furthermost reaches of time, it is inevitable that overlapping, blurring of outlines, the merging of functions and, in some instances, total expropriation will take place. For example, among some of the Altaic peoples shamanesses are found and the same goes for Korea. However, in the second case there are elements which suggest the adulteration of original Korean shamanism by other influences. In an article in the December 1977 issue of *Korea Journal*, the American anthropologist Dr Laurel Kendall describes the *mugam*, the dance in shaman's dress which forms part of the *kut*, the complicated rite of the Korean shaman. In it, an ordinary woman will temporarily take over the role of shaman and dance until she herself becomes possessed. Here we have a denial of the very ethos of the shaman for whom the embodying of the spirits is a unique prerogative, gained only through great pain and difficulty. The idea of those who had not undergone these ordeals becoming their vehicle is so unthinkable that one is bound to suspect an intrusion.

Though I believe women to have been involved in mediation with the supernatural, it was one of quite a different kind.

Female Magic

Feminine complicity with the fount of life was confirmed when women took on a new task. They became first the plant-gatherers and, later, when it was realized that, inserted into the soil, a seed would reproduce its kind, the growers.

It was the destiny of plant-derived food, especially in the form of cereals, to become and remain the most important constituent of the human diet; the bread of the growers, the women, not the meat of the hunters, was the 'staff of life'. The sustenance the female provided did not end at her breasts.

It was perhaps at this time, we cannot be sure, that the image of the Great Mother began to undergo modification. She was no longer seen as coextensive with the earth itself, but became rather as its informing spirit – the Mesopotamian Ishtar, the Egyptian Isis, the Aztec Coatlicue, the Greek Gaea, the Norse Freya, the Danu or Don of the Celts; a random few from an enormous list. Earth Mothers, but in a true sense 'fertility goddesses'.

As such they are the leading players in a group of markedly feminine myths. In them the fertility goddess sometimes has a daughter, as Gaea had Persephone, whose alternative name, Ceres, the young woman, is the root of the word 'cereal'. More often she is paired, either as mother, wife or lover and sometimes all three, with a handsome and noble youth – Osiris, Adonis, Freyr, Dionysus. In every case we have the story of his descent and rescue from the underworld by the divine heroine or of his rebirth in a new form through her intervention. Child, husband or lover, they are the vegetation gods, the informing spirits of that which grows in the farmer's fields.

On mortal women, because of their new-found importance as growers, fell the crucial task of invoking the goodwill of the Earth Mother and her divine offspring at the crises of the year, the seedtime, the germination, the harvest. Whether the growing corn was personified as a young man or a young woman, a lover was needed and must be ritually provided – perhaps the romantic novel has longer antecedents than we realize.

By the time we come to know of the Egyptians, the cult of Isis had not only been taken over by a male priesthood, but had undergone reformation and refinement. None the less, there are hints of something of a very different character. Though human sacrifice served more than one purpose, an indication that it had more than one origin, so persistent a theme of myth is the provision of mates for the gods of vegetation that it must have been one of them. Celtic goddesses were passionate and insatiable, in constant need of fresh lovers, as the queen-goddess, Mebd, confesses to her husband, King Ailill, in one of the legends of the Ulster cycle. From pagan Connaught comes the story of the maiden whose demands could be satisfied only by providing her with a man from each community, a plain hint that they were to be sacrificial victims.

In Aztec Mexico, the most beautiful girl of a town or village was chosen as the mate for the young maize-god. On the morning of his festival all her girl friends gathered at her home and there, amid much twittering, giggling and excitement, dressed her in a robe of corn yellow in his honour, coloured her face the same hue and finally crowned her with a headdress resembling the ripening cob. Then to the music of flutes and drums, she would lead the entire community in a day of dance and feasting. She was the mistress of the revels and one can see in her the original role of the British carnival and May Queens for, at sunset, she would head the procession as it threaded its way towards the maize-god's temple. There as she crossed its threshold a priest, lying in wait, would slice off her head with a single stroke, releasing her to the embrace of her divine lover.

From Greece come accounts of the rites of Dionysus who, despite his later epiphany as the god of wine, was in origin a vegetation deity. His votaries, the Maenads, mostly women, gathered in some remote place deep in the countryside where, by the light of pitch-torches and to the accompaniment of flutes and the remorseless, pervasive beat of drums, they chanted and danced until they achieved a state of frenzy such that they could tear a full grown bull to pieces with bare hands to devour its raw flesh. The superhuman strength necessary was *entheoi*, possession by the god, root of our own 'enthusiasm'.

These communal, nocturnal rites evoke obvious resonances. For example, there are the fire-walking ceremonies of India, Malaya, Japan and China which certainly have as their object the ensuring of a good harvest, but which also link with the other feminine activity, that of fire-providers. Similar customs in classical Greece survive under the auspices of the Orthodox Church.*

There is an even stronger resemblance to Haitian and Dahomeyan voodoo and the Brazilian *Candomble* cults, in both of which participants can become possessed and manifest all the classical symptoms of ecstasy, moaning and writhing on the ground with upturned eyes.

And one is also reminded of the Witches' Sabbaths as they are described not only by witch-hunters such as the authors of the *Malleus Maleficarum* but by the more dispassionate pens of men like the eighteenth-century French historian Jules Michelet.

The Displacement of the Female

A drama in which the leading characters are a woman – the Earth Mother – and a younger personage, sometimes female, but more often male, represent the obverse, the vegetative side, of the coin of human mythology, but it also has its masculine, reverse side. Here, not only is the protagonist male, but so are all the principal players. Woman, if present at all, is either a mere supernumary or else the agent of disaster, sometimes through her stupidity, sometimes through her wantonness, sometimes, like Pandora or Eve, through her ungovernable and typically feminine curiosity.

These are what might be called the myths of the 'Divine Gifts'.

In them the human race acquires something essential to its well-being or representing a watershed in its progress directly from the hands of a well-disposed deity. Metal-working, fermenting liquor, even decimal reckoning and phonetic writing are only a few of the skills thus bestowed. These are the myths of Prometheus, of the Celtic *Tuatha de Danann*, of Quetzalcoatl, of the Hindu Purusa – all beings much like the shaman himself, and in at least one case, that of Odin, actually so called.

The division of function between the sexes might seem to have much to commend it. One of the duties of the shaman was to conduct the dead to their new homes, so here was an arrangement whereby woman, the life-bringer, stood guardian at one portal of human existence and man at the other. Nothing

* In 1981, a group of British tourists, attending such a ceremony, convinced themselves that a trick must be involved and the coals on which the faithful walked barefoot could not really be hot. They took off their own shoes and joined in. Their holiday ended in hospital where they had to be treated for serious burns.

could appear more ideal and harmonious.

In fact it was neither. On the part of the shaman, there was a profound and remorseless antipathy to the feminine and no opportunity to oust or vilify it was neglected.

Of course, as child-bearer, woman was willy-nilly a rival. Yet it was not her terrifyingly and enviably potent magic which posed the real threat. It was the communal nature of the rites of the Earth Mother and her divine offspring, with possession open to any or all, which menaced the elitest and individualistic shaman.

And it is in the light of this that we can understand why the female had to be displaced wherever and whenever possible. Eliade points out that feminine deities play only a minor role in the pantheon of the shamanistic Turko-Tatars. The Yakuts have no representation of goddesses and a similar state of affairs is found among other Siberian peoples where female divinities are restricted to the guardianship of the child-bed.

Often, too, the shaman gave his enemies female form. From wherever he is found come stories in which he is in conflict with the malign and powerful woman. Rasmussen's Eskimo informant tells him that among the things his people most feared was Takanakapsaluk, the Great Woman who lives at the bottom of the sea and rules over all marine creatures. The Norse Underworld was ruled by a queen, Hel. In Greek Orphism, notably antifeminist in its ethos, the Underworld is the realm not only of its king, Hades, but also of Persephone. When the Lapp shaman descended into the Underworld it was on a perilous visit to the realm of the fearsome *Jabmieakka*, queen of the dead. She is 'the thief of souls', the crime with which, down all history, woman has been charged.

That the male was victorious in this conflict is plainly demonstrated by all the world's religions, even those of the remote past. The Egyptians were an agricultural people inhabiting an extremely fertile region of the earth, exactly the place where one would expect the Earth Mother and her divine son to reign supreme. And so they do – but firmly in the hands of a male priesthood.

The Celts were agriculturists of a high order, credited, among other things, with the invention of the iron plough. In some of their myths the feminine element is paramount, indicating an origin among the growers. In one story from the admittedly late Welsh *Mabinogion*-cycle, the young knight, Pryderi, ventures into an underworld castle to recover the bowl of the sun. When he reaches for it his feet immediately stick fast to the floor so that his mother, Rhiannon, has to try to rescue him. Here, then, is a myth very much in the tradition of the maternal or wifely rescuer of the young hero. Despite this, we have it on Caesar's authority that the Druids, strongly imbued with shamanism and still part shaman themselves, never lost their hold on Celtic society. At some stage in Celtic social evolution the female had been elbowed out.

In Greece, though several of their goddesses developed out of Earth Mothers, among them not only Gaea, but also Aphrodite and Artemis, religion was similarly dominated by the masculine.

Among existing religions attitudes to the feminine vary from hostility to condescension. In the *Epic of Mahabharata* of Hinduism, itself a religion strongly tinged with shamanism, Brahma creates woman 'in order to delude Mankind'. She is the epitome of evil, sharper than a razor, 'a poison, a serpent, death all in one'.

It is no different elsewhere. In the synagogue, women are relegated to seats in the upper gallery and a similar situation obtains in the Moslem mosque. The Early Fathers of the Christian church devoted much time and energy to debating whether women had souls.

Often, the shaman's malign foe is a witch. E. R. Dodds rightly describes Pythagoras as a 'Greek shaman'. Among the list of taboos laid upon his followers are a number, such as rubbing out the mark left by the pot in the ashes of the fire or disposing of hair-clippings and nail-parings, explicable only as specifics against the malevolence of witches for whom such things are essential *materia magica*. And witches' spells are, of course, the theme of one of the great comic classics of the Ancient World, *The Golden Ass*. As the work itself shows, its author, Apuleius of Madaura, was greatly influenced by Pythagorean ideas.

Another of Dodds' Greek shamans, Orpheus, placed a ban on his followers being present at childbirth. An exactly similar proscription is placed on most shamans. One can see why. Not only is this the time when the Earth Mother is most potently present, but the midwife has always been related to the witch by virtue of the fact she plays the role of assistant of the divine.

One sometimes gets the impression that shamanism was the male's attempt to neutralize the female's terrifying magic. Certainly the masculine, and often sexually exclusive, nature of shamanism is something which we shall find repeatedly occurring.

PART II: CLASSICAL SHAMANISM

3. Recruitment and Training

Although their numbers dwindle by the year, people subsisting by hunting and pastoralism are still to be found, and among many of them shamanism survives, while other nomadic peoples, such as the Lapps of Northern Europe, practised it up to fairly recent times.

This has made possible first-hand studies and, as the bibliographies of books like those of Mircea Eliade overwhelmingly demonstrate, over the past half century our knowledge of the subject has grown dramatically.

With the increase has come a revolution in attitudes, the work largely of two pioneering spirits. In 1923 the Soviet anthropologist Sergei Shirogokorov published his *General Theory of Shamanism among the Tungus*; in 1929 the Danish explorer and ethnologist Knud Rasmussen, himself partly Eskimo, wrote the work from which quotation has already been made, *The Intellectual Culture of Iglulik Eskimos*, the fruit of many thousands of miles of Arctic travelling. What marks both Russian and Dane is the abandonment of the condescension which marked attitudes of the past towards 'primitives'.

The last decade has seen another development: the emergence of a generation of trained Western anthropologists who claim themselves to have undergone shamanic initiation. They include Carlos Castaneda, Dr Leslie Gray and Michael Harner in the United States and Professor Arnold Keyserling in Vienna. Castaneda's series of books on his experiences with the old Yaqui shaman Don Juan have become international best sellers, while Michael Harner has acquired sufficient of an international reputation to have been invited to address the Soviet Academy of Sciences and is currently engaged in a project to reintroduce shamanism among peoples who have lost it, such as the Lapps and Eskimo. He has also founded his Center for Shamanic Studies in Norwalk, Connecticut, which runs training courses and workshops.

Only the test of time will show how much or little they have advanced our knowledge and it has to be admitted that they have been subjected to a great deal of criticism. Castaneda, for instance, has been accused of lack of intellectual rigour, even of purely imaginative embellishment.

Yet no amount of adverse and perhaps unjust criticism can totally detract from the value of these people's activities. Naturally, whether one regards shamanism as a collection of superstitious prejudices we should long since have outgrown or as something which has a valuable contribution to make to our understanding of the universe must depend, as much as anything, on personal attitudes, but trained minds observing its phenomena, as it were, from the inside can, in the long run, only help us to discover whether it contains nuggets of real value. For years hypnotism and herb-medicine were dismissed as primitive mumbo-jumbo and it was only when open-minded men and women began experimenting for themselves that what lay beneath the incantatory dross was revealed.

And as knowledge accumulates we can see ever more clearly that shamanism presents a consistent picture. Whether we take that of the Arctic or the Australian outback, whether we turn back the leaves of history to those whom Professor Dodds calls the 'Greek shamans', similarities in the way in which a man was summoned, how we responded to the summons and the experiences he underwent thereafter show resemblances so remarkable that we are plainly dealing with a single constellation of ideas.

The Choice of Shaman
If ever a human activity was entitled to be called a 'vocation', this surely must be it. Like the young Samuel of the Bible, one does not choose shamanism, it chooses one.

Invariably, we find that he on whom the mantle falls has been singled out, sometimes from birth, by a physically distinguishing feature such as an extra finger, a harelip or a birthmark. By the same token, the stigmata may take the form of mental or nervous dysfunction. A child who, at puberty, has fainting fits will often be regarded as a prospective shaman. So, too, will the victim of epilepsy, hysteria or the so-called 'Arctic sickness', a loss of mental balance said to come about through prolonged exposure to sub-zero temperatures and boundless snowscapes.

Naturally with epilepsy or hysteria, hereditary factors may be involved and in a few places the profession may itself be hereditary, with one family looked to to produce the tribal shamans as another will be seen as its 'royal family' responsible for producing chieftains. In exceptional cases, descent may even be in the female line. In another form of hereditary shamanism the call does not travel lineally, but comes about because the individual is thought to have 'inherited' the soul of a recently dead shaman. One is obviously reminded both of belief in reincarnation and of the method by which the Dalai Lama succeeds at the death of a predecessor, of the parties of monks searching the length and breadth of Tibet for the child who reincarnates the Dalai Lama's soul.

The choice of shaman may also take the form of an external occurrence. To the Altaians an unfailing sign is of lightning or a thunderbolt falling in front of the individual and, as Eliade points out, this is itself indicative of whence the shamanic powers are thought to come.

The Vocation of Shaman

Even where hereditary succession occurs, the spirits are regarded as the ultimate arbiters so that a particular family will be thought to produce shamans solely because it stands in a special relation with them. And the belief that he enjoys the favour of the spirits is one of the sources of the shaman's enormous power within his society.

The acquisition of such power would seem to make his vocation a highly desirable one. Indeed, if we accept that Druidism evolved from shamanism we have it on the authority of Caesar that there were always many who were eager to study it while others were sent to do so by parents or relatives. Broadly similar evidence comes from Rasmussen who mentions that Eskimos who wished to become shamans went off in search of teachers. They usually appear to have been unsuccessful and those determined enough were forced initially, to pursue their own path, as in the case mentioned in Chapter 1.

However, his power over his peers notwithstanding, the recognition that he has a vocation is by no means invariably welcome to the recipient and, though he knows it to be vain, he may well resist as long as possible.

As to the spirits themselves, they seem to favour a carrot and stick approach. On the one hand, their chosen candidate will be tempted by lavish promises; on the other he will be tormented. Ultimately, he will fall into the so-called 'shamanic' illness which may last for months or, if he continues in his obduracy, years.

Obedience to the call may actually occur during the illness itself. The candidate then falls into a coma which can last anything from three to nine days. In other cases, illness persists until the sick man surrenders.

Often one can see in the surrender the attempt to break out of a vicious circle. Thus the sufferer from Arctic sickness interprets the onset of symptoms as the call of the spirits. Dread at the thought induces nightmares which serve only to reinforce belief and his only escape is to start shamanizing. As one put it, 'Had I not become a shaman I would have died.'

More usually, however, as with Rasmussen's witness, surrender will lead the novice shaman to abandon his familiar locations and take himself off into some remote place in desert or forest, there to live off whatever nature provides, experiencing hunger, thirst and other privations. In the end he will begin to hallucinate, his delirium becoming ever more hideous until he undergoes an experience of death and dismemberment. One explanation advanced for this vivisection by the spirits is so that they can discover whether he has any extra bones in his body.

Among the Australian Aranda people, the man who feels he has been called to be shaman goes to a particular cave where he falls asleep. During his slumber the spirits will come to him, one thrusting through his neck and out through his mouth a spear which, though invisible, none the less, leaves ever after a hole in his tongue large enough to admit a finger. Some of these holes have been seen by outside observers who have vouched for their authenticity.

A second spear-thrust is fatal and his spirit is taken to the Other World, where all his internal organs are exchanged for a new set made of quartz crystal. Finally, his spirit is returned to his prone body in the cave where, in due time, he will reawaken. An almost exactly similar experience is undergone by most Siberian shamans whose body is cut to pieces by the spirits and the flesh stripped from the bones. Often it is cooked and eaten.

The process of dismemberment culminating in consumption is a plain survival from the hunting phase, since it is exactly what the hunter does to his quarry; namely, kills it, skins it, removes the offal, then cooks and eats it.

But it also has two other aspects.

First, the Other World is a reverse mirror image of our own. Rivers flow towards their source, the dead are left-handed – the probable source of the mystique and, in many instances, the prejudices surrounding the left-handed, as manifested in the word 'sinister'. At the same time, the fact that it is day there when it is night on earth is the reason why, almost invariably, the celebration of festivals took place at night. Caesar mentions the Druidic custom of measuring time by nights rather than days, a relic of which survives in our own 'fortnight' or 'fourteen nights'. Hence, among the other reversions of the Other World, it is also the place in which humans become the prey of the creatures they preyed on in life.

The second aspect is that of ensuring equilibrium. By offering himself as a sacrificial victim the shaman is repaying the debt humans have incurred by their slaughter of animals. In the words of Rasmussen's Eskimo, 'All the creatures we have to kill and eat, all those we have to strike down and destroy to make clothes for ourselves, have souls, as we have.' A clear example of the underlying concept comes from the Yakuts of Siberia where the Bird-of-Prey Mother carries off the shaman's soul, tears it to shreds and gives a portion to other spirits much as the mother falcon or eagle feeds her young.

The theme of being slaughtered, cooked and eaten, then reborn occurs in many myths. Among them are the Orphic Rhapsodies, the 'scripture' of the followers of Orpheus, where the evil Titans seduce the child-god Dionysus into trusting them by giving him pretty toys and having done so kill and eat him. Zeus, enraged by their cannibalism, struck them down with his thunderbolt. What remains of the unfortunate divine child is then taken by Apollo to be reconstituted.

Transformation

During his sojourn in the wilderness with its accompanying hardships, the tyro shaman will have undergone a transformation in his modes of perception. 'The only true wisdom lives far from mankind, out in the great loneliness, and it can be reached only through suffering,' Rasmussen was told. 'Privation and suffering alone can open the mind of man to all that is hidden to others.' It is thus he gains 'the shaman's light of brain and body', perceptible to the 'spirits of earth and sky and sea' and which allows him to see through life's darknesses. In similar terms another informant, this time a Siberian shaman talking to

Shirogokorov, speaks of acquiring the power 'to see with closed eyes into darkness, into hidden things, or into the future or into the secrets of another man'. As Campbell puts it, he can now 'see through veils' and both Castaneda and Harner speak of their instructors as seeming to possess a contact with the very forces informing the universe.

Initiation and Ordeal

As with every other detail of the shaman's calling, the death/rebirth cycle, though constant, shows regional variations, so that in some places it is reduced to the symbolical form of an initiatory rite. In others, the extreme opposite applies and the candidate may have to undergo ordeals of an extremely painful nature, either self-inflicted or inflicted by initiators.

Beatings, burning with fire, slashing with knives, suspension often upside down from a tree for hours or even days, ascending a ladder of upturned sword blades are all to be found. One Eskimo candidate spent thirty days naked in a snow hut, fed by his master only on occasional sips of warm water. Often he felt he was dying.

In some cases these experiences are additional to that of dismemberment by the spirits. In others, he may cut off a finger offering it as a kind of gift in exchange for secret knowledge or he may inflict tortures upon himself, as in the case of an Assiniboin shaman who cut off strips of his own flesh and fed them to snakes. It is in terms of such mutilation as a form of barter with the spirits that we can interpret Odin's offering of his eye for one sip from the well of Mimir which gave arcane wisdom.

However, even the crisis phase is not universally regarded as necessary or else it may take place only symbolically. In a form of initiation practised in some parts of Mongolia and among the Tunguso-Manchurians the future shaman is ritually introduced to the spirits of the Other World by the elders. He then scales a pole or stake erected for the purpose, his action representing a spiritual ascent to the Upper World.

A Sign of Rebirth

As a measure of the fundamental change which has taken place in him – his 'rebirth' – the neophyte shaman will often change his name. The Christian baptism itself, as the Book of Common Prayer avows, is a form of rebirth and is also the time when a child is given its name.

In other cases, the shaman's conversion may go even further and he may change his sex. Although probably more common in the past – Herodotus tells us that the Scythic Enarees were a 'class of effeminate persons' – among people where it still occurs are the Kamchadal, the Asiatic Eskimos, the Koryaks, as well as some Indonesian, South American and North American tribes. Eliade mentions it in respect of the Chukchee who have a special class of shaman said to exchange their male for female sex as a result of an instruction given to them by the spirits.

The Shaman's Familiar

Whatever the form of his initiation, now able to reach the spirits, he begins to form an intimate, lifelong relationship with his own familiar. While, as one would expect, in societies where totemism rules, the familiar will be an animal, it is also quite usual in those which have adopted anthropomorphized deities. Castaneda's mentor repeatedly refers to 'power' – that is to say Other World – animals who assist him in his work and they also figure in Harner.

Normally the familiar will be of the opposite sex to the shaman and, since, as we have seen, the male tends to predominate in the calling, is usually female. Indeed, it may be less helper than a celestial wife and, when he is in her presence, he always emphasizes her superiority in every quality to his earthly spouse. Thus the Teleut shaman, quoted by Eliade, addresses her as 'My darling wife', adding that his mortal one 'is not fit to pour water on thy hands'.

However, the true shaman's association is more than a marital partnership between mortal and spirit-animal. He can himself become an animal, even taking on the form of spirit-helper. Lapp shamans could turn themselves into wolves, bears, reindeer or fish; those of Semang, Sakai and Kelantan into tigers. Transformations into flying squirrels would be consistent with the flight metaphor of the shamanic trance, as would the birds found in Mongol, Arctic, Indian, Oceanian and American shamanism.

The Lore of Shamanism

Having emerged from the first, ecstatic phase of his initiation, the new shaman now passes on to a second, that which Eliade calls 'the traditional one', the induction into the lore of shamanism at the hands of an instructor.

Usually, as with the Aranda shaman of our earlier example,

his teachers will be other, older members of the profession. Again the pattern is by no means invariable, for his further training may take the form of instruction from the spirits themselves. In any case, if we are to go by Castaneda's account, trance-induction continues right through his training and it is at this time that he acquires his song as the call to his spirit-guide. This may take either the form of the particular creature's cry or may introduce the cry into it, perhaps in its choruses.

Instruction, always oral, is intensive and prolonged, though the twenty-year novitiate Caesar tells us that what the student Druid had to face may be excessive in the case of most shamanistic systems. Almost certainly much of it would have consisted of myth learning, but it would also have covered practical topics such as plantlore and, especially, the gathering and preparation of the sacred herbs – that is to say, the hallucinogenic substances. Despite the fact that Harner initiates his student shamans without recourse to drugs, there is no doubt that their usage is deeply entrenched. Indeed, his own first experience took place after drinking a decoction made from the *ayahuasca* or *quechua* vine, nicknamed 'the Vine of Death', said to make those who take it clairvoyant.

Castaneda is persuaded by his mentor to experiment with three substances – Jimson weed, *Datura stramonium*, which is related to our familiar potato, a smoking-mixture based on a fungus and called '*humito*' (meaning the little smoke), as well as the button-like fruit of the peyote cactus. The being who manifests himself to Castaneda while he is under the influence of the last is given the name of *Mescalito*, recalling that peyote is the source of mescalin known to us in its synthesized form as LSD. The peyotism to be found throughout Central America and even in some parts of the United States, in fact, represents a whole range of cults, including some Christianized ones, all marked by shamanistic influences.

Among other substances undoubtedly used to assist trance induction is the *Soma* of the Indian Brahmins, probably extracted from the resin of the eastern Mediterranean pine, *Ephedra fragilis* and the Haoma of the Persian Magi. Pythagoras is said to have taken something called *Kykeon* (meaning disorder), while the Thracian shamans of the first millenium BC inhaled hashish.

Among other intoxicants must be included the comparatively innocuous alcohol, especially in the form of mead. Knowledge of its manufacture was acquired and passed on to humanity by Odin who stole it from Asgard, the dwelling place of the gods. Similar divine origins attaching to mead in the mythologies of both India and Greece hint at its original use as a ritual drug and the recurrence of the bee goddess in the cult-art of the Old Europeans of the Balkan area strengthens the belief. It is also possibly significant that among the Aztecs alcohol was permitted only to the priesthood and the old.

However, a list of hallucinogenic substances with possible shamanistic connections is so endless it would require many pages to complete and would have to include the so-called 'hard drugs' – opium and its derivative, heroin, as well as less common ones such as the tobacco juice of the Jivaro Indians of Ecuador and the extract of the takini plant used by the Carib shamans of Dutch Guiana.

Most common of all were the substances extracted from the various forms of fungus. We know that the Lapp shamans chewed the toadstool *Fly Agaric*. Since this has a red cap flecked with white and gives the sensation of flying it has been most persuasively argued that it may have been the source of the stories of Santa Claus in his red cloak. Eliade speaks of ecstasy induced by this means as being known through Siberia, and its history can certainly be traced back at least 6,000 years. Although some authorities believe that the Druids used an extract derived from the poppy and hence related to opium, it is equally probable that they used the so-called 'Magic Mushroom' found in Wales and so much desired by the hippies of the 'sixties. Marija Gimbutas suggests that the frequency with which representations of mushrooms occur in the Vinca art may well have been because of its psychomimetic qualities.

In all cases, we find the harvesting of these potent substances accompanied by meticulous ritual and carried out under strictly controlled conditions, while the same scrupulously observed rituals also attended their preparation and consumption, an indication that their effects and the risk from abuse were fully understood.

Breath-control

Besides drugs, in many places the novice shaman would also have been instructed in the techniques of breath control, another widely used aid to trance-induction. Eliade connects it especially with Indo-European shamanism and it certainly lies behind yogic practice. Onians in *The Origins of European Thought about the Body, the Mind, the Soul, the World, Time and Fate* claims that in many cultures the lungs were regarded as the 'seat of the senses'. The Greek word *phrenes*, actually means 'lungs', but is sometimes used to signify the soul. As he points out it is plainly cognate with the Hindu *prana*, meaning breath, but especially the vital breath, that which imparts life to the body.

However, breath control is not exclusively Indo-European, for practices in which its use is involved are to be found in many divergent and geographically separated locations. A number of observers have remarked on the shamans' practice of panting like an out-of-breath athlete for some time before and as they went into trance. According to Needham there is a parallel in Chinese Taoism. Both Christian and Jewish mystics employed a technique of 'overbreathing', that is to say taking quick, shallow breaths. Among initiated Kabbalists it was used as part of a meditative system which induced a trance strikingly like the shaman's ascent-journey.

The Novice Shaman

Having digested all this information, final 'graduation' could be marked in one of a number of ways; for example, by some public ceremony in which the shaman is introduced to his people. Often animal sacrifice is involved and the new shaman may be expected to give a demonstration of his skill. However, among other practices to be found is that mentioned by Dioszegi in which the novice takes part in a ritual combat with an elder of the calling.

Ake Hultkrantz cites an instance* in which two shamans, or *noiaidit*, got drunk, quarrelled, and then challenged one another to a magic duel. Defeat in such a contest was, we are told, disastrous for it meant that the *noaidi's* helping spirit had itself been vanquished. From now on he could expect his reindeer to die or abort, his fishing and hunting expeditions to be unsuccessful and, in the end, he could even die himself.

This dual, though by no means of universal occurrence, obviously recalls that of the priests at the sanctuary of Nemi mentioned by Frazer in *The Golden Bough*. Here the candidate for the priesthood succeeded to his office only by killing the current holder of the office. He retained it until such a time as, his vigilance slipping, he was himself slain.

We may also have hints of something like it in the contest of

---

* His source is Nicolai Lundi Lappi, *Descriptio Lapponiae* (Svenska Landsmal XVII:5, Uppsala 1905). Nicolai Lundius was himself a Lapp.

the two magicians which occurs at the beginning of the Irish myth-cycle, the *Tain Bo Cualnge* (meaning Stealing of the Bulls of Cooley).

4. Equipment

Before he begins to practise, the new shaman will have to set about obtaining the various items of equipment essential to his activities. They include a caftan or robe, headgear, and in some, though not all cases, a mask and footwear.

Most important of all, there is his drum.

Although there is what might be called a 'standard' shamanic costume, the variation found from region to region is considerable. Indeed, in some places he functions naked, while Louise Backman and Ake Hultkrantz are of the opinion that, with the Lapps, special apparel was not regarded as at all necessary. They suggest that items labelled as noaidic costume in the museums of Oslo and Stockholm are likely to belong to a late phase when the calling was in decay and the noaidit were trying to impart respectability to it by emulating the vestments of the clergy. There are even cases, such as among the Eskimo, where even the drum is missing.

The nude *noaidit* would appear to be in minority among shamans, however. Usually, clothing is regarded as so integral to their operations that even naked ones will have some item such as head- or arm-band, a belt or no more than length of cord without which they cannot function. Costume, as Eliade points out,

> constitutes a religious hierophany and cosmography ... Properly studied it reveals the system of shamanism as clearly as do the shamanic myths and techniques.

Hence, the shaman's costume will be decorated with symbols associated with his vocation and whose purpose is to identify him to the spirits, to help him gain power or to protect him from Other World enemies. They may include representations of snakes, lizards and frogs, as well as the sun, moon and planets or the organs of the body, including the sexual ones, and various items may be made from metal or from bones, sometimes from the human body. Among those who adopt this somewhat macabre form of adornment are the Tofalar, Soyet and Darhat shamans, though bones, of course, have a special significance in that they are regarded as providing the raw material for the resurrection of those who had died or been slaughtered, a motif found in many myths and, *inter alia,* in the Biblical dream of Ezekiel. We have already noted the custom in hunting communities of preserving the bones of a slaughtered animal and returning them to a place frequented by its species.

Other figures which may be incorporated are depictions of birds, particularly aquatic birds such as the gull or the swan, indicative of the shaman's association with water.

In addition, other embellishments are likely to include coloured ribbons hung from the waist and down the back, or from the skirt of the caftan. These are known as 'snakes' and the resemblance is increased by forming their ends into the shape of a reptilian head. An Altaic shaman may have over a thousand such 'snakes'.

Altogether all this ornamentation can weigh as much as fifty pounds (100 kilos), a statistic which gives some measure of the sheer physical energy required for the shamanic seance.

Since the shaman wears it exclusively while invoking the spirits, his costume comes to be their abode. When an item wears out, instead of discarding it, he will hang it on a forest tree to allow it to depart in its own time. Among some of the Tungus tribes, after the death of the shaman, his costume is kept and observed carefully to see whether its inhabiting spirits manifest their presence by making it move or shake.

The shaman's need of a special costume in order to operate is reminiscent of the robe traditionally associated with the magician, particularly in folk myth and fairytale and the similarity is increased by the fact these were normally decorated with the signs of the zodiac or the alchemical symbols for metals. The portrayal of the magician in children's fairytales derives from Renaissance engravings and there is no doubt that the Renaissance mage regarded a costume, made from special materials and ceremonially donned as essential.

The Caftan and Cloak

The equivalent of the traditional magician's robe is a cloak or caftan. Sometimes, as with Goldi-Ude shamans, this is worn over a special shirt or with an apron; in others, it is put straight over the naked body.

It may be made from any one of a variety of materials, but that of the Altaic shaman which is made from goat or reindeer skin may well represent the oldest and best preserved tradition, recalling as it does the skin-covered sorcerers of the cave drawings.

The principle of contact with the animal world is involved in those cases where the shaman wears over his caftan a cloak or cape often made of the cured skin of an animal of the same species as his familiar. Where the actual skin of the species is not used, patterns embroidered or painted on the cloak will be intended to represent it and in the comparatively few instances where the familiar is a fish or reptile, scales will be represented in this way.

The same goes for bird familiars, where actual feathers may be sewn on the cloak or depicted in embroidery or paint.

Such ornithological symbolism is frequently found, with birds of prey and, especially, the eagle among the most popular. This, the 'King of the Birds' is, of course, also repeatedly found in mythology. The Celtic solar deity Lugh takes on the form of a bird in one story, while a bird is also linked with Zeus. Odin becomes an eagle in the myth of his theft of mead, and the fact that in *Rig Veda* Soma was said to have reached humanity through the mediation of a supernatural eagle suggests a common origin for both Scandinavian and Hindu myths. Among other peoples, the Buryats and the Yakuts believe the father of the first shaman to have been an eagle.

The Pectoral

In addition, some wear as a 'pectoral' a polished disc of metal, usually copper, 'the shaman's mirror'. It serves a number of roles. By gazing into it the shaman will be able to see the hidden secrets of the future, but there is also evidence that it was used to frighten off evil spirits who, seeing their own hideous reflection, fled from it. The mirror of the Buryat shaman was decorated with the representation of twelve animals, which suggests a zodiac.

Intended for a similar purpose and obviously linked to the crystal-gazer's ball are the pieces of quartz crystal used principally by the shamans of Malaysia and the Americas. We have already seen how the Australian aboriginal had his intestines mystically converted into quartz.

According to Harner all these peoples consider quartz crystals 'the strongest power object of all'. (By contrast, Eliade says they play no significant role in Siberian shamanism.) Among reasons for its importance Harner suggests quartz's power to refract light, but he also points out the enormously important role played by quartz in modern electronics. The word processor on which I am writing these words has, as its fundamental constituent, the microchip, actually a form of synthesized quartz.

The Mask

Another item of costume, though one less commonly found, is the mask. This may resemble the 'Devil masks' of such places as Polynesia, but in other locations will represent or may be made from the head of an animal or bird. The Buryat shaman's equipment included a monstrous mask made of hide, wood or metal and adorned with an enormous beard. Black Tatar shamans occasionally wear a mask of birch bark with eyebrows and a moustache of squirrel fur.

A more rudimentary form is that adopted by the Goldi shaman who simply daub their faces with suet, and such use of fat is found in several other places. This has led to the theory that the mask is intended either to frighten off unsympathetic spirits or as a simple disguise to prevent recognition, while others suggest that it evolved from the blindfold once worn by some shamans during their seances.

Both are plainly over-simplifications and the history and form of masks as found in various parts of the world makes it plain that they serve several purposes, including that of making the wearer recognizable to those spirits with whom he wishes to communicate, accounting for the use of masks made from the head or face of a particular species or which imitated it in some way.

In assessing the significance of the mask we have to consider its two aspects, which might be called its objective and its subjective effects. Inspiring dread or providing an identity falls into the former category since this is the effect it is intended to produce upon the beholder. The subjective effect is that which the mask has upon the wearer himself. He is believed actually to become invested with its personality in the same way that the mask or *persona* enabled the Greek actor to achieve *mimesis*, the process by which he actually becomes the character he is portraying.

We also know that in some societies a mask will represent an ancestor and the wearer will then become his or her incarnation.

Eliade, citing Harva* suggests that the comparative rarity of the mask is accounted for by the fact that the shaman's entire costume is in a sense a mask, fulfilling the requirements of making him identifiable while, at the same time, enabling him to take on the personality of another creature.

Headgear

The feather motif found in the cloak is often repeated in the headgear, those from the swan, eagle or owl being the most popular and usually incorporated complete with wings. Like the feathers on the cloak, symbolic of the shaman's 'flight', they bring to mind other flying creatures, namely the angels of Judeo-Christian mythology, as well as the winged helmet worn by Hermes/Mercury. As we shall see they are not the only link this particular god has with shamanism.

In some places headgear consisted of a bear's head, though horns in one form or another appear most frequently. These can be from an actual animal, such as a span of reindeer antlers mounted in such a way that they can be worn on the head, or can be made of some material such as iron, which itself has strong shamanistic associations. Eliade quotes from a Buryat shaman's 'Manual' which describes a cap made of iron bands and which incorporates horns.

Campbell even mentions an instance† of an old Yakut who claimed that, in his youth, shamans used to grow 'pure, opaque' horns with which they would imitate the bull, presumably in their more playful moments.

Onians reminds us of the special sanctity attached to horns in the Ancient World. The reason for this was that the brain was actually regarded as the soul and as the procreative element (seminal emissions were widely regarded as coming directly from the brain and travelling through the bones, as it were, through a system of pipes). Thus, in Minos and Mycenae horns were regarded as a sort of spiritual outcrop. It is for this reason, the author suggests, that the words for brain and for horns are similar in so many languages, as, for example, the French *corne*

---

* Harva, Uno, *Die religiosen Vorstellungen der altaischen Volker*, Helsinki, 1938.
† His source is Ksenofontov, G. V., *Legends of the Siberian Shamans*, Munich, 1955.

(horn) and *cerveau* (brain), or the Greek *keras* and *kara* (head and skull). One cannot help suspecting such beliefs originated in shamanism.

Footwear

If headgear played a vital role and shows considerable uniformity, footwear is a more haphazard matter with some shamans going unshod. In those regions where special footwear was necessary it could represent the hooves of a deer, a bird's claws or the paws of a bear as portrayed in the engraving of a Tungus shaman in an eighteenth century Dutch travel book, *North and East Tartary*.

As to the manner in which he is to possess himself of each item of clothing, this will come in a series of dream instructions. In some cases he will purchase them from the family of a dead shaman paying with a horse, a creature traditionally associated with shamanism and with the sun.

The Drum

Despite the Eskimo exception, the item of his equipment regarded by shamans almost universally as being of unique importance is the drum. In either its customary form or in one so modified through the centuries as to have made it unrecognizable, the drum is constantly associated with the magical, further confirmation of the belief that magic has its roots in shamanism.

Its purposes are manifold. In many places it is used to summon and hold the spirits during divination and healing, though in some cases, especially in South and Central America, the shaman may generally use a rattle – the prototype of the *maraccas* beloved of the Latin American orchestras – for these purposes. Harner discusses the use of the rattle in his own practice, in particular in shamanic healing, and gives his students instructions for its employment.

But, more importantly, the drum is a vehicle by which the shaman makes his journey to the Other Worlds and is spoken of either as 'the shaman's horse' or, if he has to cross the waters, his 'boat'. In one case the drumstick will be his lash; in the other, his paddle.

However, sometimes, as among the Yurak of the tundra, the drum is called the 'shaman's bow' or his 'singing bow'. One explanation advanced for this is that the drum was originally used to drive away evil spirits, that is to say, like the archer's bow, it served as a weapon. The real answer may well be that the bow served to project an arrow which flies through the air as the shaman is thought to fly during his journey. Thus, the drum becomes the means by which he is projected and, in fact, we have examples drawn from many societies in which the shamanic flight is actually likened to that of an arrow. Among them there is, of course, Apollo, according to Eliade 'the most shamanistic of all the gods'. One of his many titles is *Hecatebolos*, the shooter from afar whose silver bow looses its golden arrows, and a 'golden arrow' was the vehicle on which Abaris, the mysterious 'priest of Apollo' associated with Pythagoras, was said to travel.

But the singing bow may also have another basis. With some kind of sound-box attached to it, the archer's bow becomes a rudimentary musical instrument and, in fact, the bow used for playing the violin and similar instruments is a relic of this. In any event, we know that some shamans, such as those of the Kirgiz, used a stringed instrument rather than a drum to induce trance.

While the drum in itself implies a link between shamanism and music (a question discussed later), the use of stringed instruments helps to support it.

★   ★   ★

Though there are instances of double drums, such as those of Tibet, usually the drum is single sided and more often oval than round. It is held in the hand, sometimes by means of a single band of leather across the back of the frame or by two crossed straps forming an 'X' or, in rarer instances, a 'Y'.

Its frame is always believed to be derived from the wood of the World Tree, that which, standing at the centre of the world, is its axis and the point of junction between lower, mortal and upper worlds.

Where hereditary shamanism rules, the drum will pass from generation to generation and, among shamans with large families, each child will take a turn at playing it until one of them exhibits the ability to shamanize.

But how is it obtained in the first place? Irrespective of whether the family or other kinds of shamanism are involved, the method of acquisition is much the same, that is to say it is a matter in which the guidance of the spirits is sought.

Among the Ostyak-Samoyed, the shaman will find the correct wood by going blindfold into a forest. The first tree he touches will be assumed to be a scion of the World Tree from which a branch is cut for the frame. Among the Altaians, the information as to which tree to use will be conveyed in a dream and the shaman will direct his assistants where to find it.

But before laying axe to branch, it is necessary to placate the tree's spirit and this is done by anointing it with animal blood or alcohol.

The Drumstick
Scarcely less important than the drum is its stick which will be of wood or horn with its beating surface covered in fur. Sometimes it may have rattling rings hanging from it. The power of the drumstick is such that it may itself be used for divination, as among Tungus shamans who use it to answer questions by throwing it up and determining the answer from the way it falls.

Not only its gathering, but everything connected with the preparation of the drum and drumstick will be attended by ritual. The drum skin, usually that of a reindeer, elk or sometimes a horse, will be decorated with human and animal figures, sometimes on both sides; sometimes only one. Similar designs will also be drawn on the drumstick.

Before it can be used, the drum must acquire a soul. The Altaians animate it by sprinkling beer first on the frame, then on the skin. Imbued with life the frame will then tell the shaman the life history of the tree from which it was hewn. Having been duly asperged in its turn, the skin will give a biography of the animal which provided it, ending with a promise to serve the shaman faithfully.

This animation process may take the form of a seance in which the spirit of tree or animal speaks through the shaman who, in the case of the animal, imitates its cries and behaviour. As most authorities stress, the spirit of the drum is actually that of the most powerful of all the shaman's helpers.

Despite the use of the drum as an aid to trance induction, in some places it has undergone considerable modification in the course of its long evolution. Often, for instance, it will be no more than a wooden hoop without a skin at all. In others, the hooped shape itself has been lost and it has become simply a staff or wand, though even in this highly abstract form it is still regarded as having come from the World Tree.

We may well suspect that what we have here is the ancestor both of the traditional magician's wand as well as the hazel-fork of the dowser or water-diviner. The traditional woods of the latter are willow, because of its connections with water, rowan and, especially, hazel, which were also those favoured by shamans.

Notwithstanding the loss of its conventional drum form, the staff remains 'the shaman's horse', and like a horse, it is ridden astride, the possible origin of the witches' broomsticks. At the same time, since the staff was frequently decorated with a carved representation of an equine head, it can also be taken to be the original of the mummer's Hobby Horse, probably itself the prototype of the walking sticks with horse's heads carved on their handles which turned the late Victorian and Edwardian working-man in his Sunday best into such a dandy.* In fact, a horse-headed stick actually occurs in some shamanistic contexts, such as among the Buryats, Javanese and Balinese.

The shaman's 'horse' has other echoes. While it might be extravagant to imply that every knight of every courtly romance is a shaman in disguise, those of Arthurian legend could well have been something very close, that is to say disguised Druids, the subterfuge being necessary to avoid the Church's proscription on paganism. A number of commentators have pointed out that the topography of the legends, with their dark, impenetrable forests and mysterious castles strongly suggest the Other World and so lead to the suspicion that this is what the writer is seeking to portray. In some of the stories, such as the early Welsh one of the young knight Pryderi and his mother Rhiannon, suspicion becomes virtual certainty for Rhiannon is the specifically Welsh form of the Celtic mare-goddess known elsewhere as Macha and Epona. Although unrecognized as such by the monkish redactors, she is, in fact, only one among the scores of Celtic deities who appear in the Welsh stories, further indication of their provenance.

That the Arthurian knights are actually Druids would be of a piece with the shaman's description of himself as a 'warrior', that is to say a warrior dedicated to the struggle with Other World forces. It is precisely what Castaneda's Don Juan most often calls himself.

★　　　★　　　★

---

* They are still being made and sold. I myself came across a stand at a Sussex crafts' exhibition where they were on sale.

Now ready to practice, the new shaman knows, none the less, that he stands on the lowest rung of his profession which is, in any case, hierarchic, dividing its practitioners into small, intermediate and great. According to both the Tungus of eastern and the Yakuts of north-eastern Siberia, the souls of future shamans repose in nests among the high trees of the Upper World. Those in its topmost branches are the greatest with various lower degrees occupying descending positions. (It is in the light of this that we should perhaps consider Caesar's reference to an 'Archdruid', a sort of Druidic Pope, a concept which has always been accepted with some reserve.)

Despite this pre-natal determination of status, it is quite plain that in real life, the shaman will depend far more for success – and no doubt survival – on his personal dominance over his peers, his native wit and, perhaps most important of all, his histrionic talent, since a shamanistic seance is, above all, a dramatic presentation. Nor is there much doubt that when his own paranormal gifts failed or were regarded as insufficient he was not above resorting to conjuring tricks to sustain his reputation.

5. Functions

Dioszegi says of the shaman that he must know everything necessary to humans in their everyday life but which the ordinary individual cannot know through his own capacities. Ake Hultkrantz, whose studies have been restricted mainly to the Lapps, describes the shaman as having five main functions: those of healer, of psychopomp or conductor of the dead; of animal-charmer, of prophet and of sacrificial priest.

The Shaman as Physician
As physician, the shaman's responsibilities will extend not only to sick humans, but, if they are pastoralists, to his people's livestock.

Like any other doctor, his first task is that of diagnosis. Illness may be caused by tormenting spirits entering the body, by the soul straying from the body, or by its falling into the hands of hostile spirits.

Having decided on the cause, he must set about remedying it. Where invasion is suspected he will summon the aid of his assistant and together they will enact a mime to draw the intruder from the patient's body.

In this connection, Joseph Campbell quotes from a work by E. Lucas Bridges, the son of a missionary among the Ona people in what is now Ushuaia in the south of the Argentine. Bridges describes how, kneeling beside the patient, the shaman first used his hands as though to gather the source of the illness into one place, then applied his mouth to suck it out. This could go on for as much as an hour until finally he moved away, his hand over his mouth as if holding something in it. He would then spit out a gobbet of mud, a stone, even a tiny mouse.

As the son of a Christian missionary, it is only to be expected that Bridges's attitude to what he witnessed would be scornful. Michael Harner, equally predictably, gives a somewhat more sympathetic account. He himself practises 'sucking' medicine, and describes the process in some detail. It consists of first locating the place of the intrusion, which is done in a kind of light trance, then having found it, invoking his spirit-helpers and, with their aid, sucking it out as in the manner of Bridges's Ona shaman.

Harner also cites the account of a female Indian 'sucking doctor', Essie Parrish, herself a convert to Christianity, though she seems to have practised her skill even after conversion. She relates how, in her early career, the diseases she exorcised would take the form of something like a bubble or a balloon in her throat.

The second cause of illness, soul-loss, comes about because the link between the mortal and immortal parts is easily broken. When rupture occurs the disembodied soul (like the shaman's in trance) wanders abroad, as also happens in sleep, for instance, or when someone is unconscious. Like any wanderer, the errant soul can get lost, and the body, thus deprived, sickens. The only solution is for the shaman to seek and restore it.

But the journeying soul can suffer worse fates than losing its way. It is highly vulnerable to the machinations of ill-disposed spirits and can, as it were, be kidnapped, as happens to Castaneda in *The Teachings of Don Juan*. Again the only person capable of restoring it is the shaman. The task may well involve him in just the kind of desperate spiritual battle of which Castaneda gives us intimations. Backman and Hultkrantz tell us how noiaidit, called on for the service, were compelled to venture into the dangerous realm of the Queen of the Land of the Dead.

Although his success as communal physician depended primarily on his ability to master the spirits, there is no doubt that in most cases it also included herb-medicine. That the effectiveness of cures was regarded as depending less on the pharmacological properties of the plants themselves than on the formularies attending their gathering and application is again clearly shown in Castaneda who describes his drug-gathering expeditions with Don Juan. He is simply echoing what we already know from the folk-medicine of most peoples. Typically, the patient or his relatives will be instructed to pick a stipulated number of specimens of the healing plant (usually three or nine) under a new or full moon, and following a precise ritual, prepare an infusion which the patient is to take under similar strict conditions. Only if all the details are scrupulously adhered to will recovery take place.

Usually, the shaman-doctor's task will not end with cure, however. The patient and his family will be anxious to insure against relapse and it is for the shaman to make certain that the spirits have been thoroughly propitiated. Frequently, as with the north Siberian Ostyaks, animal sacrifice may be called for, in which case he will decide on the number to be slaughtered.

Among many peoples, such as the Goldi of the Amur region of north-west Asia, a shaman will also be consulted when a woman is barren and, in trance, will ascend the tree of souls to send down an embryo.

Although in general they shun childbirth, in some areas shamans are called upon to be present at it and, even where they are not, may be consulted to discover whether the expected child will be a girl or a boy and to make the appropriate ritual preparations to bring about a safe and uncomplicated delivery. We are told that among the Lapps and Koryaks it was customary to sacrifice a dog for this purpose, while among the Buryats, the shaman performs the post-natal libations necessary to ensure the infant does not cry and to help speed and assure its healthy development.

Psychopomp

If he is not invariably present at birth, the dying will certainly require the shaman's offices. Not only will he direct the memorial rites, but, as among the Goldi, will attend at the deathbed of a tribal member or as soon after death has taken place as possible in order to catch the departing soul and lead it to its resting place, the road being, as Eliade points out, thoroughly familiar to one who so frequently travels it. Actually, the word 'road' requires broad interpretation because often it is water that must be traversed, as in the case of some of the Indonesian peoples and among the Dyak of Borneo.

The shaman makes the crossing, not only in the interests of the deceased, but also of his survivors, for if not safely delivered to his future home, he will continue to haunt his earthly one.

As to his actual post-mortem fate, a great deal will depend on the manner of his passing. A violent death is regarded as equivalent to an initiation, causing the soul to rise to the Upper World, obviously a precursor of an idea prevalent in some cultures even today – that death in battle, for instance, is immediately rewarded in the after life. The Norse Valhalla, the

Hall of the Brave, presided over by Odin, is an example of the principle which is to be found in many mythologies and, in view of the shamanistic characteristics of gods like Odin, it is hardly surprising to find them fulfilling the role of divine psychopomp.

Death by fire, especially if the body is consumed, is another form of initiation, for the soul, like the shaman's in trance, rises with the smoke. What we may also have here is the basis of sacrifice by burning as, for example, practised by the Druids at Beltaine (meaning The Fires of Belenos) on the 1 May, as well as of the cremation of the dead found in so many places.

In contrast, those who die from illness are believed to be destined for the underworld. The reason is that illness is thought to be caused by underworld spirits, though it has to be remembered that, to shamanism, this is not necessarily a place of torment.

In Christianity the shamanic function of psychopomp has, of course, been taken over by the priest, and nowhere is this better exemplified than in Greek Orthodoxy where it is believed that the soul of the dead remains attached to the body until released by the priest at the funeral mass.

Master of Animals

Humans have hunted for a longer period of their evolution than they have pursued any other activity and an indication of the influence it has exerted is the persistence of hunt metaphors and themes in so many connections, including mythological ones. One thinks of the hunt settings in which so many of the Arthurian legends are placed, while an 'other world' hunt is to be found in the folklore of many peoples, including the British, even today.

It is, therefore, only to be expected that it is among the hunters and fishers that the shaman's services should be regarded as most essential. His forecasts on the prospects for expeditions will be vital and, in consultation with his spirits, it will be for him to advise on where the largest concentrations of animals are to be found. According to Backman and Hultkrantz, the forest Lapps of Finland believed their shamans had the power actually to summon the herds of wild reindeer to the group's own hunting grounds.

Certainly wherever the shaman is to be found in a hunting environment, he is regarded as possessing skills far greater than those of the normal woodsman or tracker, and these may well include the ability to converse with birds and animals in their own languages. To Eliade the gift is synonymous with the shaman's 'spirit' language, that in which he addresses his familiar, but we have numerous examples of the shaman communing with the animals, birds, and even fish he encounters in everyday life. Among the characters in *Kulhwch and Olwen* is Gwrhyr Interpreter of Tongues, one of two Druids who accompanies the adventurers and who, in the course of the tale, seeks directions from two owls, an eagle, a stag and a salmon.

But the shaman can also change his own form into that of an animal. Thus, the Lapp noiaidi could turn himself into a wolf, a bear, a reindeer or a fish, Eskimo and Chukchee shamans into wolves, those of Semang, Sakai and Kelantan into tigers, while the Druids, too, were credited with shape-shifting.

The belief that human beings could transform themselves into animals persisted until as late as Renaissance times with men like Giovanni Batista Porta, colleague and friend of Galileo, actually describing in his *Naturall Magick* how it could be brought about through the use of hallucinogens.

The Prophet

In regard to his people's own herds and flocks the shaman's duties will not be limited to curing their diseases. Left to his arbitration, too, will be many other decisions, such as when they can safely be moved from winter to summer pastures.

At the same time, apart from the normal crises of life, there are, of course, the greater catastrophes which can befall the community – those of earthquake, tempest, drought. As prophet he will be expected to predict them but, when he fails, it will be for him to find out the cause and to seek to prevent its recurrence.

His advice will be invoked before any major enterprise, such as a mass migration or a war with neighbours, deciding the propitious moment for its launching and laying down the rituals to ensure the goodwill of the spirits.

As diviner, the shaman may reveal the unknown past or future and in some cases, such as among the Altaians, is believed to have the ability to influence the outcome of events or to determine the weather. Rain-making is a skill still associated with the shaman, particularly, though not exclusively those of the Americas.

The Sacrificial Priest

As we have seen, it is for the shaman to decide how many

animals must be slaughtered to requite the spirits once a sick man has been restored to health, while among many peoples such as the Altai Kizhi, every disaster that strikes an individual or community is regarded as being due to the activity of a *kormos*, a displeased dead soul. When it occurs, it is the task of the shaman to discover which particular kormos is responsible and determine the sacrifice necessary to appease it.

But, notwithstanding such examples as these, most authorities believe that it is only in exceptional circumstances that the shaman plays the part of sacrificer. Shamanic sacrifice is, in any event, quite different in character from that which we find taking place at the great annual festivals of the formalized religions such as those of, say, the pre-Colombian civilizations. Indeed, in those societies where they actually take place he may not even be present and, if he is, serves what Eliade calls a 'spiritual' role in that he performs the initial purifications rather than the sacrifice itself.

None the less, exceptions in which shamanic rites involve sacrifice are to be found in many societies and there is no reason to doubt that in earlier times the victims of these were often human. Among the Batak people of Sumatra, for instance, the preparation of the shaman's staff or wand could call for the offering of a child whose soul was to be incorporated into it. The Druids usually buried a child in the foundations of a new building, a custom probably acquired from earlier inhabitants of the lands they occupied and, in Britain and France, the custom survived in modified form until late times, for the excavation of mediaeval buildings has frequently brought to light the remains of a young animal buried when the foundations were laid. An example is to be found in the Aitre St Maclou, the sixteenth-century charnel house of Rouen. The body of a kitten disinterred there is now on display in a glass-fronted box at the entrance.

However, all these are very specific uses of human sacrifice and it is debatable whether such things as the holocausts mentioned by Caesar in which scores of victims were consumed in the wickerwork effigy of a man could be said to be strictly shamanistic. Data drawn from surviving shamanism suggests that most commonly sacrifice involved animals – chickens, goats, pigs or lambs. Where it was not carried out for such purposes as propitiating the spirits after recovery from illness, the offering might well form part of the consecration ceremony, as with the initiation of shamanesses among the Chilean

Araucanians, or it may be connected with the setting up of the pole or stake on which the shamanic ascent will be made.

Eliade describes in detail the horse-sacrifice carried out by the Altaian shaman as a preliminary to this. The horse symbolizes both the sun (in the case of the Indo-Europeans) and the life force itself – as we saw, horsehide was one of the materials used to provide the skin of the shaman's drum. This probably accounts for the occurrence of horse-sacrifice in so many contexts; for instance, among the Kumandin of the Tomsk region of Siberia and the Buryats. Herodotus tells us that the Persian Magi, a distinctly shamanistic body, sacrificed white horses to their river gods.

Traces of horse offerings are even found well into the Middle Ages, the thirteenth-century Gerald of Wales describes how the ceremonies surrounding the installation of a new king in the Ulster town of Kenelcunnil included coition with a mare which was subsequently slain. In India similar practices were known from earliest time, though here it was the queen who performed a simulated sexual act.

In the Altaic case it is plain that the soul of the sacrificed horse serves as a ghostly mount for the shaman on his Other World journey and one may well assume a similar rationale behind most such instances.

Shaman as Lawyer

One will seek in vain for an ethical code in shamanism. There are, it is true, places in which the shaman acts as a kind of moral instructor, though always and only through his familiars. Lewis discusses the Zimbabwean Korekore, a Shona sub-tribe, in which the shaman, as mouthpiece of the spirits, will launch into exhortations to eschew the sins of adultery or homicide and will urge tribal members to live in harmony one with another. But such examples, though by no means unique, are untypical.

Nor, as we have seen, does the shaman regard disaster as punishment for sin or as signifying the breaking of divine ordinance. He deals with each specific instance by providing rituals suited to the need and differing with the occasion. Naturally in tribal life some events take place at regular intervals – the animals come into season, mate and bear their young – and the rituals the shaman prescribes to ensure that each passes off successfully may well become established as part of a tradition. Thus, the Lapp noiaidi will always carry out his sacrifice in the same way, cutting off a piece of the animal's ears and rump while it is still alive and presenting them to the god. Finally, he will slaughter the animal and daub specially appointed stakes with its blood. The other remains are then eaten by the assembled company including the noiaidi himself.

None the less, even if shamanism provides no moral code, the most rudimentary society needs regulation if it is not to degenerate into anarchy. For instance, the human reproductive urge has to be regulated, a need which has led almost every society to surround sexual activity with complex taboos. There are besides the problems involving, if not property, then the ownership of goods and chattels and their partition at the death of a tribal member. Unless controlled these would inevitably arouse socially disintegrating family quarrels.

It is the shaman who normally provides the regulatory mechanisms in the form of tribal laws whose original source will have been its totem which he alone is qualified to consult. Gradually a body of precedent and interpretation will be built up, passed on orally from one generation to the next. Relics of the practice to be found in Brahminism are mentioned by Weber and it survived among the Brehons, the body of travelling lawyers found in Ireland until their extirpation by Queen Elizabeth I, as well as in the Manx 'Breast Law', a wholly oral system which, until recent times, took priority over codified statute.

Other Functions

His juridical function is only one of those he occupies by virtue of the fact that he is the 'memory of his people'. He is also their mythologue and epic-singer. Lucas Bridges, cited earlier, says of the shaman with whom he became acquainted that he spent much of his time chanting the mythological lore and legend of his tribe which, the author wryly comments, 'he seemed to prefer to work and drudgery'.

We have already associated the shaman, not only with the drum, but with other musical instruments. Most plucked instruments were probably devised and originally employed by shamans, a fact commemorated in the myth of the invention of the lyre by Hermes and his presentation of it to Apollo, patron of the arts through the Muses from whom the word 'music' derives.

And it is this selfsame instrument which we have found serving him as the means of trance induction which was also the accompaniment for his myth-singing. The harp-strumming

Celtic bards, mentioned by several of the classical writers, were originally Druids and reverted to many of their Druidic activities, especially in Wales, after the Roman ban on Celtic religion.

Another role ascribed to the Druids, that of instructor of the young, also has parallels in the shamanism of many societies.

Since he was custodian of the sacred myths and master of the rituals, particularly those which ocurred annually, the shaman had also to be keeper of the tribal calendar. In its most primitive form it need have been no more than a notched stick, though there is little doubt that the recognition of the relationship between the passing of time and the movements of the heavenly bodies, especially the sun and moon, must have occurred quite early. Hence, we find astronomy figuring in his activities.

Shaman as Smith

We have not yet examined the admittedly controversial question of whether the shaman functioned as a smith. The differences between normal shamanic activity and metalworking are, of course, considerable. The latter is the manipulation of physical materials by physical means and, while the shaman certainly operates on and through the material, it is usually by non-physical means. Furthermore, unlike the shaman's, the smith's skill is usually hereditary and requires no preparatory ecstatic experience.

Nevertheless, as Eliade points out, the fact that so many of the themes of shamanism are to be found in the mythology of the smiths must lead to at least the suspicion that they were originally a single body. An example is the eagle which, among the Yakut, as among many other peoples, is associated with both. According to a Yakut proverb 'smiths and shamans come from the same tree' and the use of iron in the shamanic costume and, in a few instances, for his horns are further links. In many cultures, too, the smith is accorded the same deference as the shaman and even thought to have the power of interceding with the spirits.

And it is surely significant that just as the other sciences are associated with the shaman, so metallurgy springs from magical beginnings in alchemy. What is more, the smith-gods of most pantheons – Hephaistos, Thor, Govannon, Vulcan – bear a strong resemblance to the Gods of the Divine Gifts. Like Prometheus, Quetzalcoatl or Odin, they communicate with humankind, passing on the benefits of sacred knowledge. Thus, the Greek Hephaistos, expelled from Olympus, set up forge and bellows on the island of Lemnos, and its principal town was renamed Hephaistia in honour of the fact that he there instructed local dwarves how to mine ore and work metal.

A similar legend is to be found among the Buryat people who believe that the sons of one of their gods came down to earth to teach metallurgy.

The shaman is connected with metalworking in another way. In many places one of his titles is 'Master of the Fire'. He can handle hot coals without getting burnt – a skill still retained by some African witchdoctors – emit flames from his body and raise or lower his temperature. These skills obviously recall the Tibetan practices, described by writers such as David Neel, in which lamas proved their ability by breaking the ice on a lake, dipping a blanket in it, then drying it with the heat of their own bodies. This, in its turn, reminds one of the 'warrior-heat' and 'battle fury' mentioned in Germanic and Celtic myth. It was said of the Ulster hero Cu Chulainn that, when he was in it, he could melt the snow for a yard all round him and that climbing into a tub of cold water it immediately boiled and had twice to be replenished before he was brought down to his normal temperature.

Since, for reasons stated earlier, I believe women originally to have had control of fire, this may well have been something the shamans purloined from them or cultivated as a means of demonstrating their superiority.

The Shaman and the Paranormal

From the foregoing the one indisputable fact to emerge is that the shaman's province is what we should today call 'the paranormal'.

One can go further and declare that all the phenomena associated with the paranormal can be found in the shamanistic context. He is clairaudient, that is to say, able to hear voices. He can change his shape, alter his body weight – making himself featherlight or rock heavy – a gift also associated with certain Spiritualist mediums and Tibetan lamas. He can render himself invisible. He can fly. He can 'bilocate' or be in two places at the same time.

He is also clairvoyant, using his skill, among other things, to find lost objects or strayed animals. Frequently, as with prophecy, clairvoyance will call for trance, though in some cases dream or visionary experiences may be involved, sometimes after taking a hallucinogenic drug.

Eliade regards such 'minor exploits' as clairvoyance as being the prerogative of shamanesses, but Tornaeus, quoted by Hultkrantz and Backman, speaks of Lapp shamans seeing things which were happening 'in remote places' and there is little doubt that such abilities were taken for granted among shamanistic communities.

★   ★   ★

The shaman's wide-ranging functions and the skills necessary for their execution would in themselves ensure that he enjoyed enormous respect among his fellows. But infinitely more important than any of these and the source of a power and a prestige which often amounted to dread was the belief that his constant, invisible companions were powerful spirits.

Often awe spilt over into antagonism, compelling the shaman to live apart from the community as a hermit. Indeed, some societies expected him do so. Jean Markale points to the frequent incidence of hermits in Arthurian myth. They are, of course, Christian hermits in this case, but he takes it as evidence that many Druids also probably lived deep in the forest.

However, the selfsame powers which could arouse dread could also be the means of obtaining temporal power. Dioszegi mentions a Tungus shaman who, in 1752, was also clan chief and in some parts of Mongolia shamans headed clans and even tribes. Much the same was true of certain of the Samoyed and the Eskimo of North America and Asia where the words for 'shaman' and 'leader' are cognate, while the Celtic chieftain Diviciacus who addressed the Roman senate in 60 BC, may well have been a Druid.

Even where shaman and chieftain remained separate, the latter often seemed to hold his position by permission of the latter. Of King Conchobar of Ulster, for instance, we are told that he did not speak until his Druids had first spoken.

We also, and again perhaps not surprisingly, find them playing a military role. Shamans of the Evenki people who lived on either bank of the Yenisey River frequently led their people in tribal wars, while in the struggles of the Buryats against the Russians in the seventeenth and eighteenth centuries, the warriors were commanded by shamans. The Irish Druid, Cathbad, mentioned in the Ulster Cycle, was not only the father of the king, Conchobar, but had himself been a warrior as his name, one translation of which would be 'Battle Raven', indicates.

PART III: SHAMANISM AND ITS BELIEFS

6. The Shaman's World-View

In Chapter 1, we characterized shamanism as primarily a mode of apprehension, so how exactly does the shaman perceive his environment? To look for an integrated philosophical system would, naturally, be in vain, no only because shamanism exists as manifestations occurring in a diversity of regions without connections between one another, but also because of its very nature. On the other hand, since shamans everywhere fulfil much the same functions and fulfil them in the same way, can it be that there is something approximating to a world-view?

As one of the shaman's activities is that of mythologist our best hope of finding out must lie in this direction and, to be sure, from an overall examination of the myths and beliefs of various peoples common images which show shamanic influences begin to emerge.

However, we have to keep in mind that mythologies are themselves ultimately governed by the modes of thought obtaining at the time of their inception. That the mental processes of those from cultures we might regard as primitive are no different from our own has repeatedly been shown by the speed with which they can master our technologies and compete on equal terms. Eskimos or Australian aborigines can fly aircraft or programme computers as competently as Europeans, sometimes more so. And what is true of the present is patently also true of even the remotest past. A Mesopotamian priest might have subscribed to beliefs we should regard as sheer superstition, but could cope with mathematics as complex as our own and, skilled in the use of the abacus, would probably leave us far behind in the speed with which he carried out his calculations.

What actually limits all views of the universe is the human

inability to form concepts except in terms of the familiar and concrete. And what is familiar and concrete to those who see their environment solely through the medium of the unaided senses will manifestly be different from that seen by those with electron-microscopes, radio-telescopes and space-probes.

It is this and not lack of mental sophistication which leads the yurt-living nomad to believe that the universe itself is simply an infinitely vaster yurt. The same process of reasoning makes the Samoyed call the Pole Star 'the Sky Nail', the hook from which the celestial canopy hangs, while the Lapps, Finns and Estonians all used similar everyday images. Even among the great civilizations of antiquity, such as the Egyptian, informed by precise astronomical knowledge, the vault of the sky is depicted as the naked body of the goddess Nut with whom her husband and twin brother, Geb, the earth tries unsuccessfully to mate.

By the same process of extrapolation, the dramatic manifestations of nature, the daily rising of the sun, the storms, the cycle of the seasons, the growth of the crops, the erupting volcanoes, will be attributed to the activity of agents, supernatural and all-powerful, but not otherwise different from those humans saw and heard round them daily. The sound of an earthquake resembles the pounding feet of an angry bull. Hence, to the highly gifted Minoans, living in an earthquake belt on the island of Crete, the constant subterranean rumblings which were an accompaniment to life were caused by a divine, underworld bull who, because of his potential for harm, had to be gratified. The queen, Pasiphae, offered herself as his sexual mate. However, so the myth went, their union produced only the Minotaur, half human and half bovine, but who, no less capricious than his sire, required the annual sacrifice of seven Athenian youths and maidens to placate him.

The threat to Minoan existence from the underworld bull was different only in kind from those menacing other societies, and all find mythic reflection. Nomads, such as those of the Siberian steppe, lived out their lives poised on a few temperate and habitable plateaux surrounded by desert or snow-clad mountain ranges whose climate would frequently overwhelm them, causing enormous hardship and misery. The early city-states, like those of Sumeria, conceived and planned as the microcosm of the universe itself, were regarded by their inhabitants as islands in a sea of menace and hostility. So the mythologies of both Siberia and Sumer speak of the formless, the realm of creatures so malevolent and fearsome that their mere description strikes chill, as lying beyond the limits of their own domains. The same mythologies contain graphic and terrifying accounts of what will come to pass when, as is inevitable, these demons gain the upper hand.

For the Norsemen, who knew something of the savagery of the elements, the horrors of *Ragnarok* include a bitterly cold winter which follows when the wolf Fenrir swallows the sun. Having thus gorged himself, he next turns to the moon and soon the stars themselves begin to topple from the sky. The earth is shaken by tremors of such magnitude that the mountains collapse. The power of the magicians – mortal or divine – broken, the hideous, fanged monsters, jaws agape, will tear themselves free of the chains by which they have been safely fettered to roam the world, raging and devouring.

The literature of ancient Iran also speaks of a terrible winter during which an elect of men and their beasts will be saved only by taking shelter in the sheep fold of Yima, the son of the sun.

For the Aztecs, cataclysm threatened every fifty-two years, the term of their solar epoch. When the sun set on the last day who knew if it would rise again or whether the world, men and beasts would fall into the grip of an icy darkness?

Soustelle describes the gathering of anxious crowds up the slopes of the sacred Mount Uixachetecatl and how the priests scanned the sky night long, lest, as in Ragnorok, the stars themselves began to gutter out and the swarming monsters left their lairs. Then, at the precise second, the victim would be seized, flung across the altar-stone while the obsidian knife hacked through rib-cage and into the chest cavity. And as the firestick was spun in the gaping wound, the sun's first rays blazed like fingers over the mountain's peak. The sacrifice had been accepted; the world had been saved once more.

That the origins of these eschatological myths are shamanistic is abundantly clear from hundreds of instances now collated. When Michael Harner was on his first shamanic journey after taking the *ayahuasco*, he found himself in a deserted place, a surrealistic expanse beside a dark sea. Rising from its horizon he could just make out what were at first small black dots. Gradually the dots grew larger, finally to resolve themselves into huge, pteradactyl-like creatures flying on creaking, leathery black pinions. Skidding to a landing in front of him, they told him they were 'the true masters of the Earth'. Later, relating his experience to his instructor, the older man ridiculed their inflated self-description. 'Oh, they're always saying that,' he said. 'But really they're only the Masters of the Outer Darkness.'

★   ★   ★

As a matter of fact, and despite our advanced technology, we still tend to express our concepts in terms of the familiar. Unable to describe – because we do not adequately understand – the operation of the processes involved, the models used in atomic physics or molecular biology, for instance, often owe more to the imagination than to objective data.

If challenged we, no less than the shaman, might well answer that, for practical purposes, understanding and accurate representation are less important than the ability to predict the behaviour of natural forces.

And in the matter of prediction, the shaman seems to be notably successful. Certainly one of the capacities which impressed outside observers, even the most sceptical, was his quite extraordinary rapport with the natural elements. It was as though he was constantly aware of invisible emanations from animals, plants, trees, even from rocks and running waters, surrounding, even permeating him and it was perhaps because of this that Eskimo shamans have often proved far more accurate weather-prophets than the scientific meteorologists at Canadian government weather stations.

In the depths of the forest the hunter-shaman will assert he can hear or smell the presence of an animal, often describing his colour or some peculiarity at distances so great that others, particularly if they happen to be Europeans, are left incredulous. Only when the creature appears, perhaps hours later, and is seen to coincide exactly with the description will they begin to question their own judgement.

One is reminded of the statements by shamans quoted in Chapter 1: 'I could see and hear in a totally different way. I had gained . . . the shaman's light of brain and body . . . I could see through the darkness of life'; 'The world seem less foreign, more familiar; things just seemed to fit together more in every way.'

It is this 'fitting together' of every component in the environment which most characterizes the shaman's perception. Others, namely ourselves, may pay lip service to the unity. We talk of 'eco-systems' and of the network of life. We have begun to recognize that, for example, the destruction of rain-forest in one distant region of the globe produces its disastrous consequences thousands of miles away. The difference is that the shaman appears literally to 'sense' these effects. It is not by chance that Rasmussen's informant speaks of 'the shaman's light of brain *and body*'. He is no longer a separate entity, but a dynamic part of the biosphere, related to it as his organs are related to his own body and, as he senses their malfunction, so, too, he senses it in the environment.

The belief, like all beliefs, is not without consequences. To extend the metaphor of the human body: if the universe is a living thing, then every entity within it will be related to the whole as limbs and organs. And, as the efficient functioning of the body is conditional upon the efficient working of each of its components, so the macrocosm itself has to be maintained in a state of equilibrium.

The idea is, of course, inherent in the Indian concept of *Dharma*. Interpreted by Buddhists as the 'Law of Cause and Effect', it teaches that no act, however trivial, takes place in isolation. No matter how tiny the pebble, the ripples it sets up will radiate outwards to the very margin of the pond. Every cause, by affecting the macrocosm, not only reaches back to the causer, but to others as well.

In slightly different form it is also present in Chinese Taoism. To the Taoist the entire universe, including the human individual, is a vortex of energies and rhythms – the Tao – which are in a constant state of flux. The life-task of the individual is to become attuned to these, both in himself and in the external world.

This, in its turn, brings to mind the Greek idea of 'Cosmos' where again the universe and everything in it is perceived as a total unity. Although the sixth-century sage Pythagoras is credited with coining the word itself, it was implicit in the philosophies of his predecessors, Thales, Anaximander and Anaximenes, each of whom put forward different theories about its nature and the world-substance of which it was believed to consist.

★　　★　　★

But it also has another consequence. Aware of the total interdependence of the universe in all its parts, much of the shaman's effort is directed towards ensuring that every endeavour is brought into alignment with the Cosmos. It is for precisely this reason that he is consulted before all major undertakings.

He also knows that, like the pecking bird which starts an avalanche, the ordinary individual will often fail to realize how considerable a convulsion his seemingly insignificant acts have produced. The shaman must, therefore, be the utterer of warnings against the breaking of the ritual taboos, relics of which remain with us in the prohibition of bringing certain plants into a house, the supposed dangers caused by spilling salt or in the superstitions surrounding the number thirteen.

Where his warnings against taboo-breaking could not be delivered, were ignored or, like those of Cassandra, probably a shamaness herself, disbelieved, he must do the next best thing and seek to minimize the damage caused in order to save his fellows from the disasters pursuant on their inadvertent or wanton acts.

In any case, even without human assistance, the cosmic equilibrium is always in danger of disturbance. For the shaman, as for the Aztec priest on Mount Uixachetecatl, the vital and perhaps most vital task is that of its maintenance. One can see why the sacrifice of a single human life should be regarded as a small price to pay – even by the victim himself.

Caesar tells us that this was one of the Druidic uses of sacrifice and its connection with cosmic equilibrium is touched on in one of the Welsh *Mabinogion* stories. While Peredur, who is the most likely prototype for the Sir Percival of the later versions, is out adventuring, he comes upon a wooded valley, divided by a river. On either bank sheep graze. Those on the nearer bank are white; those on the farther one, black. Whenever a black sheep bleats, a white one wades through the river to join them, becoming black itself during the crossing. When one of the white sheep bleats, the process is reversed.

It needs little discernment to understand that the two fields of sheep represent this world and the Other World, and that the incident portrays allegorically the balance between them.

The Great Spirit

The conception of the universe as a Cosmos is to a great extent the pivot on which the whole shamanistic world-view turns. Order, as that within the yurt and the tribe plainly showed, was not the product of chance. What chance produced was chaos, its antithesis and the tireless enemy which threatened from without. Order resulted from the deliberate acts of reasoning minds. It followed that the order of the cosmos must be the product of a reasoning mind. Hence, the concept of the Great Spirit.

It was the frequency with which the Great Spirit was found among even remote peoples apparently untouched by outside influences which led Wilhelm Schmidt to postulate his theory of a universal montheistic impulse, later to degenerate into polytheism. The fact that his theories no longer command general acceptance does not diminish the prevalance of the belief which is to be found among the Indians of North and South America, and among Siberian peoples such as the Chukchee, Ostyak, Yakut, Buryat, Tungus, Samoyed and Turko-Tatars while at the climax of the all-important horse sacrifice of the Altaians the shaman rises ecstatically to the throne of the celestial prince, Bai Uelgaen.

In many, though not in all cases the Great Spirit is credited with the creation of the universe and with it the Cosmic Order. Where he is not, he fulfils a kind of gubernatorial role, presiding over the pantheon of deities with their various specialized functions each of which contributes to that order. He is the obvious prototype of those supreme divinities found in almost all mythologies: the Hindu Varuna, the Tiwaz of the north, the Celtic Dagda and, among the Greeks, Ouranos.

In many instances, the wide and somewhat vague nature of his functions led to his being displaced in the hearts of worshippers by those thought to be capable of intervening more directly in their day-to-day affairs. Eliade believes that the Altaian Bai Uelgaen had himself supplanted the earlier Tengere Kaira Khan and, in Greek myth, the succession of Ouranos by Kronos and Kronos by Zeus may well recall a sequence of substitutions.* Even in Vedic belief horse sacrifice was originally offered to Varuna, and only later to Prasupati and Indra.

The Centre
The dwelling place of the Great Spirit is in the celestial spheres. Hence it becomes the destination of the shaman's ascent trance. However, such an ascent would be impossible were it not for the channel of communication that exists between heaven, earth and even the underworld. This is the Centre, the axis on which the

---

* In the view of some scholars, the process had not ended with the accession of Zeus to the throne of the gods. They believe he was in the process of being displaced in favour of Apollo who, as W. K. C. Guthrie says, was the first truly Panhellenic god.

earthly disc rotates, represented in myth as a pillar, like the Ostyak World Pillar, as a sacred mountain, like the Hindu Sumeru, or as a giant tree like the Norse Yggdrasil, the ash whose roots stretched down to the land of the dead, whose branches brushed the heavens, and beneath whose shade the gods met.

Centres or their symbols are of world-wide occurrence. The ziggurats which the Mesopotamian priesthoods erected were centres. The pyramids of the Egyptians may well have been; the Aztec temples of the sun almost certainly. So was the Hebrew Mount Zion and probably Mount Sinai on whose peak Moses met God to receive the Ten Commandments. For the Celts there was a centre in County Meath in southern Ireland as well as a second at what is now Milan. In both cases, the names actually derive from a word meaning 'the centre'.

Though the Greek Mount Olympus was undoubtedly one, the Greeks had an even more renowned example on Mount Parnassus. It was, of course, Delphi, in Greek myth the omphalos or navel of the world.

Though the centre may be a single, precise location, lodes of energy spread from it like arteries. According to an old Hindu myth every mountain in the universe is connected with Sumeru, so that whenever the gods decided that a volcano should erupt or an earthquake take place, they began the process from there. Equally, the Norse World Tree, with its widespread roots, was capable of sending up shoots anywhere. It is for this reason that the shaman is able to make the stake he uses for his ascent from one of its scions.

One is reminded of the ley-line hunters' theory that the earth is criss-crossed by a grid of force-lines. It is intrinsic to it that the wise of the Ancient World, able to discover them, deliberately erected their most sacred building over the intersections, and it is an intriguing speculation whether dowsing, with its incontrovertibly shamanistic roots, may not have originated in endeavours to locate these nodes of energy.

The Magic Numbers

The centre and everything which stands for it has another association: that with the mystic numbers. The number of notches cut in the shaman's stake correspond with the levels of the Other World. Often there will be nine, while for others, such as the Ostyaks, there will be seven. The Vogul believed that a flight of seven steps connected earth with heaven and the

Mesopotamian ziggurats had the same number of storeys representing seven heavens. Plato, too, believed that there were seven spheres in the afterlife and that, through the cycle of existences, the individual should set himself the spiritual goal of attaining the highest while the same notion of seven celestial spheres penetrated the ideas of the Renaissance mages.

The number seven is, of course, one of the most recurrent of all numbers starting with the seven days of the week borrowed from Mesopotamia. Brewer's *Dictionary of Phrase and Fable* which, among others, lists the seven graces, the seven divisions of the Lord's Prayer, the seven ages of man, the seven phases of the moon, the seven bibles, the seven bodies of alchemy, the seven champions of Christendom, the seven churches of Asia, the Seven Deadly Sins, the seven joys and seven sorrows of the Virgin, the Seven Sages of Greece, the seven senses, the Seven Sleepers of Ephesus, the seven spirits before the throne of God, the seven virtues and the seven Wonders of the World, has hardly begun to make an impression on the totality.

Geoffrey Ashe in *The Ancient Wisdom* relates the preponderance of the heptad to a sacred centre lying under the seven stars of the Great Bear and, as we have seen, the Hindu world-mountain, Sumeru – home of Seven Sages – is located in this region. Eliade, while acknowledging that the seven mystique is to be found right across south-eastern Siberia, believes its wide dissemination in the west is due to Mesopotamian mediation. In his opinion the older magic number was three and the incidence of nine may come from the fact that it is the square of three. Certainly in Druidism, though seven is to be found, three is far more common and is linked with the triple deities such as Brigid as well as others who are depicted with either three heads or three faces on a single head.

For the greatest of all number enthusiasts of the west, the Pythagoreans, whose beliefs bear so many shamanistic marks, it was none of these but ten in the form of the Tetraktys, which was most sacred. The Tetraktys was a triangle built up out of the successive numbers from one to four.

The Narrow Bridge

The shaman's vehicle for his spiritual journey is, of course, his drum, which serves him as his 'horse' or as his 'boat' and sometimes each in turn.

The image of a river dividing our own from the Other World is undoubtedly the origin of those many mythical rivers found worldwide as, for example, the Greek Styx with its shadowy boatman, Charon, and the 'Jordan' of Christian mythology. Readers of John Bunyan's *The Pilgrim's Progress* will remember the summoning of Mr Valiant-for-Truth:

> When the day that he must go hence was come, many accompanied him to the Riverside, into which as he went he said, Death, where is thy Sting? and as he went down deeper he said, Grave, where is thy Victory? So he passed over, and all the Trumpets sounded for him on the other side.

Mr Valiant-for-Truth's crossing of Jordan and the shaman's boat notwithstanding, the passage over the river dividing the two worlds can frequently be traversed only by means of a Narrow Bridge. The motif is one found in Altaic shamanism, in that of Malaysia, North and South America and the Far East. Thus, in Korea, the *Mugam*, usually a woman, is called in to fulfil the role of psychopomp when someone dies. A seance or *kut* is then held at the family's expense. In trance, the mugam summons the Death Messenger who is offered various bribes to ensure generous treatment for the deceased. The mugam will also communicate with the lingering spirit of the deceased, persuading him to leave his old abode and to accept his new home and status, explaining the arrangements made with the Death Messenger for his reception.

The climax of the ceremonies is when a strip of white silken cloth is stretched between two of the mourners to serve as a bridge. The mugam splits it with a knife and pushes her own body along it, so dividing it into two narrower strips. As she does so she pushes in front of her various belongings of the dead, often including his photograph. When she reaches the further end it is believed the spirit has now been safely conducted to its new abode. The ritual ends with the destruction of the cloth bridge.

Campbell tells us that Eskimo shamans, too, had to traverse a bridge as narrow as the edge of a knife, while Eliade finds the same motif in Brahminic ritual practice, in Japanese initiation ceremonies and in Siberian and South American shamanism. He suggests that the Iranian *Chinvat peretu*, the 'Bridge of

Requittal' comes from Zoroastrianism, one of the many shamanistic traits it contains, and it may have been from them that the idea reached the neighbouring Caucasian peoples.

Chinvat peretu is not the only Narrow Bridge to be found in an Iranian context. The Sarmatian and Alani people lived near the borders with Scythia and were themselves closely related to the Scythians. The Alanis were the predecessors of the Ossetes mentioned by Herodotus and among Ossetic customs was that of the 'Horse speech', a funeral oration describing the dead man's journey on horseback to the land of heroes. In due course, this takes him to a bridge across a raging torrent at whose foot he is questioned about his past life. If it has been virtuous, he will have no difficulty crossing; if not, the bridge will collapse beneath the hooves of his mount.

The belief that the wicked are destined to fall from the bridge to be consigned to the infernal regions, sometimes a place of extreme heat, sometimes its opposite, is, of course, recurrent. Thus, the Islamic bridge *al Sirat*, sharper than a sword and narrower than a spider's thread, is impassable to the wicked, though crossed with ease by the righteous. However, the fact that in Koranic Mohammanism the bridge has been converted into a narrow path, symbolizing correct religious observance through life, links it with the 'strait and narrow path' of Christianity. Not that the Narrow Bridge itself is unknown to Christian symbolism, for it is found in the Vision of St Paul. The complimentary title given to the Pope, that of 'Supreme Pontiff', derives from the Roman liturgical honorific *Pontifex Maximus* (borne among others by Julius Caesar), and actually means 'Great Bridge Builder'.

According to some mythologies, in a long lost 'golden age' the bridge was wider and so traversible by all. In other words, in that happier epoch access to paradise was freely available, no doubt because men and women were more virtuous.

The Narrow Bridge is undoubtedly the 'razor's edge' mentioned in the Hindu *Katha Upanishad*, but occurring also in Buddhism. In Finnish folklore, the hero Vainamoinen and his accompanying shamans on their way to Tuonela, the Other World, have to cross a bridge made of swords and knives. In Norse legend, Hermod is despatched to the kingdom of the underworld queen, Hel, to beg her to free Baldur, slaughtered by the trickery of Loki. His journey takes him 'down a dark road to the land of the dead' where he encounters a bridge over the Resounding River which he must cross to reach the gate of Hel's palace.

The Ulster hero, Cu Chulainn, seeking the Amazon, Scathach, mistress of warriorcraft, crosses first the Plain of Ill Luck where men's feet stick fast and where sharp grasses spring up to cut them, then the Perilous Glens where wild beasts dwell. Finally, he comes to the Bridge of the Cliff which rises up like a ship's mast the moment anyone sets foot on it. After several vain attempts, he succeeds in crossing and reaching Scathach's dwelling.

We have already considered the possibility that the knights of Arthurian legend may be disguised Druids. The recurrence of the Narrow Bridge motif seems to me to reinforce the belief. In *Kulhwch and Olwen,* the earliest known version of the Arthurian stories, one of the characters is Osla Big Knife of whom it is related that

> When Arthur and his troops came to the cresting flood, they would find a narrow spot; the knife in its sheath would then be laid across the flood and that would be bridge enough for the three armies of the island of Britain and the three offshore islands, with all their plunder.

Chretien de Troyes is a late reteller of the Arthurian legends in whose hands they have been converted into the familiar courtly romances. None the less, his version undoubtedly contains matter lost to us elsewhere. In his *Lancelot of the Lake,* the knight, in search of the abducted Guinevere, is directed to go to the sword-bridge – so named because it is like a sword laid edgewise – which no man has crossed. Riding to it we are told that Lancelot ceased to know 'whether he was alive or dead' and even forgot his own name.

After several days and many adventures he arrives at the bridge which flows over a river 'as swift and raging, as black and turgid, as fierce and terrible as if it were the devil's stream'. And he has not only the bridge itself to contend with, for he now sees that the far shore is guarded by two fierce lions. The lions of this story are plainly a surrogate for the dogs which occur in many other contexts, as for example in Altaic shamanism, and who, one must suppose, are related to Kerberus, the watchdog of Hades.

Undaunted, Lancelot resolves to cross all the same and, before doing so, removes the armour from his feet and hands. Thus, unprotected, he passes over 'with great pain and agony, being wounded in the hands, knees and feet'. However, once on the other side he finds the lions were only figments of his own disturbed imagination.

Here we have the Narrow Bridge in classically shamanistic form. In his deliberate use of bare hands we have a plain echo of the mutilations, often self-inflicted, which the tyro shaman undergoes and, in some places, walking barefoot over upturned swords can actually figure in these. The fact that Lancelot is moving between the two worlds is made abundantly clear by the amnesia which afflicts him on his way to it. He is plainly in a trance-state.

Shamanism and the Human Personality

It is this – the trance – which is the basis of everything else in shamanism and it is largely contingent on a conception of the human personality which regards it as consisting, not of the two entities, body and soul, but of three: body, soul and spirit (a similar tripartite division is, of course, to be found among certain Spiritualists, as well as Theosophists and Anthroposophists).

Though the terms 'spirit' and 'soul' tend to be used interchangeably, the spirit could be described as the vital flame giving life to the body, but which, having fulfilled its function, is extinguished at death. For the soul, on the other hand, the body is merely a temporary dwelling which, in due course, will be vacated or exchanged for another.

Approximate equivalents are to be found in the Greek 'breath soul' or *pneuma* which, according to some writers, also perished with the body and the *psyche*, though it was only in late times and among the more esoteric sects that the human psyche was thought to be immortal. In Homeric times, such survival as the individual experienced was in a gloomy realm of dusty shadows.

As to whether it is soul or spirit which goes atravelling when the shaman goes into his trance, there is some dispute. Some say it is the spirit, which can thus be broadly identified with the 'etheric double' or 'astral body' found, *inter alia*, in Buddhism or Hinduism.

To others, however, it can only be the soul, and it is its detachment in trance which gives the shaman the appearance of being dead. Certainly, it is this component of the personality which can stray or be stolen by the malevolent. Castaneda's description of his own soul loss reflects what would be a generally held belief: namely, though that it is not immediately fatal, since the spirit ensures the continuation of bodily functions, unless it is restored, gradual and ultimately fatal degeneration will take place.

Reincarnation

I am far from the first writer to notice that those religions which include reincarnation among their doctrines invariably exhibit strong shamanistic or quasi-shamanistic marks. Among them are, of course, Hinduism and Buddhism. In Greece, where the Pythagoreans adopted the belief and passed it on to Socrates and Plato, it was probably due to the influence of Orphism.

Caesar tells us it formed part of the credo of Druidism. It is, indeed, the sole specifically Druidic teaching on whose existence we can pronounce with confidence and this absence of a doctrinal base is further evidence that Druidism was a modified form of shamanism. It must, however, be observed that for the Celts reincarnation appears to have been available only to certain of their heroes who, it was thought, would quit their tombs to succour their people in time of crisis. Relics of the belief can be seen in the legend of Arthur, once and future king, and in the Devonian folk-myth of Drake's drum which would summon him from 'the port of Heaven' should Britain stand in need of his services.

Such detectable differences in the actual form of reincarnation to be found among various peoples can be explained as the result of the separate development of a basic concept and, in spite of them, one can trace a core belief, if not once held in common, at any rate starting from the same underlying premise: that spirits evicted from their bodies by death and, particularly, by the activities of the hunter, must be seeking new homes.

In the Irish myths we have hints of it in what I believe to be an extremely archaic form. In one story the wife of the king of Ulster becomes pregnant after accidentally swallowing a bluebottle which has fallen into the cup she drinks from. The bluebottle is actually the princess Etain, earlier transformed by the spell of a malign sorceress. In due time she is reborn as her original self.

In the *Tain Bo Cualnge*, we are told that the pig-keepers Friuch (meaning Bristle) and Rucht (meaning Grunt) challenge one another to a duel of magical skill. Their rashness leads to a series of metamorphoses which culminate in their becoming maggots who fall into a spring. A cow belonging to Ailill and his queen, Medb, drinks from the spring. Like the Queen of Ulster in the story of Etain, she becomes pregnant and is delivered of two bull-calves. Hence the bulls of the story are actually the two transformed magicians.

Such myths suggest a tentative interpretation for the prohibition repeatedly found in the Ancient World against eating such commodities as beans. By the time we hear of it, from Herodotus and the classical writers on the Pythagoreans, the real basis has been forgotten and it has become no more than an empty ritual taboo. None the less, the various explanations which many of these writers advance link it with birth and reproduction. In other words, the bean, like the Ulster queen's bluebottle and the maggots swallowed by King Ailill's cow, can, in certain circumstances, actually be disembodied spirits seeking rebirth in human form.

Such stories probably predate the recognition of the male role in conception and when set against this background they are particularly instructive, for they can be seen as providing explanations of the way in which new life comes into being which cunningly avoid the painful necessity of according credit to the female.

7. Shamans Into Gods

That the rulers of the universe should originally have been thought of as animals is wholly consistent, not only with a world view which conceived everything in terms of the familiar, but with what we already know of shamanism and its roots in the hunting phase.

But, what is more, to the generality of men and women it must also have appeared as only logical that they should be animals. There was, for instance, the enormous strength of the bear, the bull, the bison, the mammoth as compared with their own puniness. There was the amazing ability of the bird to fly or of the fish to live in its aqueous element, abilities no mere human possessed.

None the less, the picture changed. Gods in human guise replaced the totems, a step in human cultural development so enormously important that the reason for its occurrence is of vital interest.

According to Eliade, the first gods were shamans. That this is an over-simplification is proved by the archaeological evidence for, as we have seen, representations of Earth Mothers are roughly concurrent with the cave drawings with their hunts and their shamans.

Naturally, the change could have taken place when increased mastery of their environment, bringing with it increased confidence, led humans to realize that they were the true lords of the universe and, hence, to conceive gods in their own image.

Alternatively, the migrations of hunters or nomadic pastoralists could have brought them into the midst of populations practising sedentary agriculture and possessing anthropomorphic deities. This is how Demeter is thought to have been introduced into the Olympian community, for she was originally

the Earth Mother of the agricultural Pelasgians, the autochthonous inhabitants of what came to be Greece. Thus, she is
present only *after* a population movement.

Equally, it could have been that the hunters, the men,
gradually took to copying the women, the planters, who had
always portrayed their divinities in human shape. Such a process
of slow emulation could account for the evolution shown in the
Egyptian iconography whereby animal-headed god becomes
complete man.

On the other hand, this cannot have happened with the Celts.
As Markale points out, they possess no Earth Mothers,
indicating that the cult of the agriculturists never took root
among them so that they had no models for copying.

It is plain that such goddesses as are to be found in the Celtic
pantheon derive not from Earth Mothers, but totemic animals.
Epona, known in Ireland as Macha and in Britain as Rhiannon,
was clearly once a mare. As Macha she is compelled by the
Ulstermen to compete in a race though far gone with child. She
gives birth on the race-track and, to avenge the humiliation,
condemns the men to suffer the pangs of labour, thereby
incapacitating them when enemies threaten. As Rhiannon she is
punished by her husband for her negligence in losing their
newborn son by being forced to carry visitors from the
gate-house to the palace on her back. Both myths echo Celtic
history, for in their original homelands in the Danubian basin,
they had been pastoralists associated particularly with horse
breeding.

In any case, interpolation and emulation can, at best, offer
only partial answers, for there is plain evidence that the
Indo-European peoples, ancestors of the Celts, had already
begun to develop gods in human shape *before* their migrations,
that is to say while they were still at the pastoral-nomadic stage.
There is a root *Deiwo* from which most of the god-words, such
as the Sanskrit *Deva*, the Latin *Deo*, the Greek *Theos* and the
French *Dieu* derive, while all have gods with similar functions
and attributes suggesting a single origin. Indeed, the French
scholar George Dumezil claims to have isolated a group of three
types of deity common to all the Indo-European peoples, those
of magic, war and fertility, corresponding to the three classes of
society, shamanistic, knightly and agricultural.

The way in which anthropomorphic gods evolved among the
Indo-Europeans was no doubt paralleled in other cases.

Lord of the Animals

In the 'twenties archaeological excavations began at a series of mounds on either side of the Indus River, upstream of its estuary on the Arabian Sea. They revealed the existence of an advanced civilization which had flourished from about 2500 to 1500 BC. Among artefacts brought to light were thousands of soapstone seals, on two of which were engravings of horned figures seated in the yogic or 'lotus' position and surrounded by animals and serpents. That they are representations of a god – probably the same one – is shown by the presence of two worshippers on one of them. The deity involved has been taken as the prototype of the Hindu Shiva-Prasupati.

The Gundestrupp Cauldron, undoubtedly Celtic and dated to the second century BC, consists of a copper vessel with embossed panels on which are the figures of gods. One is also horned, also seated in the yogic posture and surrounded by animals. In his left hand he holds the torc: in his right, he grasps a ram-headed serpent of which he is plainly the master. The same figure has been found in over thirty sites in Britain, Ireland, France, Northern Italy, Rumania, Germany and Spain. In two places he is called 'Cernunnos', a name which incorporates the word 'horn'.

Nor is his presence restricted to epigraphy. He is to be found in the mythology of both Ireland and Wales. In the *Tain Bo Fraech* (meaning The Stealing of Fraech's Bulls), the eponymous hero invokes the aid of one Conall *Cernach*. In the quest for the missing animals, as well as for Fraech's wife and children, abducted at the same time, they travel as far as the Alps where it is discovered that all are being held prisoner in a fortress guarded by a serpent of whose power and savagery they are warned. However, when they make a foray against the fortress, Conall immediately overcomes the reptile which lies in his waist belt until they have succeeded in their mission. He then releases it and, so the storyteller says, 'neither had done harm to the other'. Professor Anne Ross perceptively observes that the incident causes one to wonder whether the legend of St Patrick clearing the snakes from Ireland did not have an earlier, pagan exemplar.

In one of the tales of the Welsh *Mabinogion* cycle, Owein, a young knight, hears of Kynon and his search for combat. At a castle he is told of an adversary worthy of his mettle, but first he must seek a black giant with one foot, a single eye and an enormous iron spear. He is told, 'He is the keeper of the forest and you will see a thousand wild animals grazing about him.'

Kynon goes on his way and duly encounters the giant. Retelling his story, he says,

> My host had said he would be big, but he was far bigger than I expected . . . I greeted him, but he replied uncivilly, so I asked him what power he held over the animals. 'Little man, I will show you,' he said, and he took his cudgel and struck a stag a great blow so that it roared; with that the wild animals came until they were like the stars in the sky, so that there was scarcely room for me to stand among the serpents and vipers and animals of all sorts. He looked at them and ordered them to graze, and they bowed their heads and worshipped him, as obedient men do to their lord. Then he said, 'Well, little man, you see the power I hold over these animals.'

Both Conall Cernach and Kynon's black giant are plainly supernatural beings. In the case of the latter, as dweller in the depths of a forest where he is master of the animals, we have the counterpart not only of the Indus Valley figures, but of the Greek Pan, of the British Green Man, of Jack-in-Green, of Herne the Hunter – the name also contains a horn element – and probably of Robin Hood. In Russia, so Frazer tells us, he is known as 'Green George'. That he is not restricted to the Indo-European peoples is shown by his occurrence in other places, among them Sumatra, where the Gayos people seek the permission of an unseen 'Lord of the Forest' before venturing into it to hunt deer, wild goat or pig.

The quality of greenness, so often attributed to him, comes from the clothes made of leaves he is supposed to wear, and an early Chinese drawing shows just such a figure, bearded and leaf-covered. Among some people his skin itself has the texture of a greenery.

And we do not have to dredge the brackish pool of prehistory to find him. In a diary entry dated Friday, 6 July 1962, Carlos Castaneda relates how he and Don Juan went looking for mushrooms and were led deep into countryside which, if very different from the forests of Celtic myth or the jungles of Sumatra, remains the haunted, isolated habitat of the shaman. In fact, the hunt turns into one for the peyote cactus which leads them into a canyon where they spend the night. The following morning they consume peyote buttons and Castaneda begins to hallucinate. When his chaotic fantasies have subsided, he finds himself back near the canyon. And there he sees Mescalito, the peyote god. He is green with a skin like the surface of a peyote plant.

That we are dealing with shamanistic creatures in each of

these instances is manifest, not only from the incidence of horns in so many of them, but also from the presence of the snake. The creature is invariably associated with the feminine principle; first, because it lives in holes in the earth; and, secondly, as Alan Bleakley points out, because it regularly sheds its skin as the woman sheds the lining of the uterus. Thus, the shaman's mastery of the snake is also his mastery of the feminine.

Reading the accounts of Kynon's encounter with the giant, one naturally thinks of the Finnish Lapps' belief in the power of their shamans to summon the herds of reindeer to the tribal hunting-grounds. And, of course, all these figures correspond with the shaman in one of his most typical guises: that of Lord of the Animals which, as it happens, is just what the Hindu Shiva-Prasupati is called. It is illuminating that he is linked, especially, with the Brahminic or priestly caste.

What we seem to have in Shiva-Prasupati, in Cernunnos, in Conall Cernach, in Kynon's giant and the Forest Lord of the Gayos is the shaman himself become god.

How did his deification come about?

Quite simply by his passing permanently on to an Other World, already his second home. There he would have become available to his living successors, as one might say a 'helper' in human form. Indeed, we know that in some parts of Siberia the shaman's spirit helper was, in fact, a former shaman. Obviously the more powerful he had been in his lifetime, the more his passing would be mourned by his fellows and the more likely they would be to seek him out in his spiritual home.

But the process of anthropomorphization, having begun with the shaman, would be likely to extend itself to the other spirits. The shaman's animal 'helpers' would themselves, and no matter how slowly, begin to take on human characteristics or oscillate between these and their original animal ones. So we have Epona/Macha/Rhiannon who, though a woman in the myths as we have received them, shows plain signs of an equine past.

Shamanic deities

If my hypothesis is correct then we should be able to find, in most pantheons, deities who bear shamanistic characteristics and who give evidence of being or having once been 'Lords of the Animals'.

It is exactly what we do find and we first encountered them in Chapter 2. If one takes a broad overview of the temperaments of the gods, they seem to fall into categories. There are those who as far as they deign to notice humanity or its cares at all do so only with amused contempt, the ones of whom Shakespeare can say, 'As flies to little boys are we to the gods'. In contrast with them are those who pass their wisdom on to humankind, sometimes defying their fellow deities, even those more powerful than themselves, to wrench benefits for the race which, in some cases, they are actually credited with founding. A few are even said to be the creators of the earth itself. They are, of course, the Gods of the Divine Gifts and when one scratches the surface many reveal themselves to be Lords of the Animals. One need only go a little deeper to detect, as in a flaking fresco, the likeness of the shaman.

Traces can be made out in the Mesopotamians' Marduk or in their sun-god Shamash. Besides being solar in character, Shamash is a god of justice, for nothing can hide in the sun's brilliant light. He is the ruler of oracles through which the future is revealed. He has also been a shepherd, a calling which in some respects makes its holder a Lord of the Animals. In any event, it is one from which a disproportionately large number of mystics down to recent times have come and it is not difficult to see how the solitary hours spent with his flocks would afford the shepherd ample opportunity for contemplation, perhaps shading off into trance.

But examples of the shaman-god as divine benefactor and as universal creator are seen most clearly in the cosmologies least influenced by the great religions or the great pagan pantheons. In some cases, it is true, the work of creation is attributed to a Great Mother, but in most of those societies where shamanism is deeply entrenched, that is to say among the hunters or wandering pastoralists, one finds the deified shaman in the role of friend of humanity. For example, according to the myths of the Ostyak people who inhabit the banks of the Yenisei River in Siberia the entire creation is the work of the Great Shaman Doh. Hovering over the waters with a company of waterfowl and finding nowhere to rest he orders a diving bird to go to the bottom and bring up a little mud. Its tiny beak can hold a mere grain, but out of it the Great Shaman makes an island which, spreading like algae over the surface of the water, becomes the earth.

Not far removed from the shamans and perhaps even descended from the Great Shaman Doh are the Apache gods known as the Hactcin of whom the most powerful is the Black

Hactcin. He is the creator of all life, an act which culminates in his fashioning the first man and woman.

Various writers have found shamanistic traits in three of the principal Hindu gods, Varuna, Mitra and Indra. Indra, it is true, destroys the dragon Vritra which might suggest a shamanic, serpent-slaying role, but in this case there is no hint that the dragon in question has a feminine connection.

Verethrghna, sometimes, though on little evidence, regarded as the Persian counterpart of Varuna, is another dragon-slayer and the fact he is represented both as a white horse, identified by the Persians with the sun and, like Apollo, as a handsome youth might seem to support the view that he has a shamanistic ancestry. Though it is rare to find shaman- and war-god combined, the fact that Verethrghna plays such a role does not necessarily disqualify him. On the other hand, his shamanic links are so tenuous that it is difficult to make a positive declaration.

A far more shamanistic Zoroastrian god is, to my mind, Ahura Mazda. We first know of him as god of the Achaemenian kings (sixth century BC), though he was a great deal older than the dynasty, for there are Assyrian references to him at least two centuries earlier. The Achaemenians were Medes and already practising Zoroastrianism at the time they absorbed the outlying provinces, unifying the country into what we now know as Persia and thus introducing a single religion into this larger area and extending the cult of its chief god. The etymology of the name is disputed and among interpretations advanced for it is 'wisdom', from the Sanskrit *medha*. The most convincing one is that it comes from *Mada*, the radical which yields 'mead' the intoxicator. Mazda's connections with shamanism were increased when, under the Sassanian kings, he reverted to being what he had probably been originally – a god of priesthood.

Mazda is not only the creator of the universe but the giver of five marvels intended to provide humanity with pleasure and solace, but into each of which the evil spirit, Ahriman, injects the canker which will ultimately destroy it.

Among the pre-Colombian civilizations of Central America, Quetzalcoatl, the Plumed Serpent, and the most universal of all the gods of the region, also shows a number of shamanistic characteristics in that he is the benefactor of humanity, bringing to it the arts of cultivating maize, weaving cotton, polishing jade and making feathered mantles (the last strongly suggesting the shaman's garments). He is also humanity's instructor in calendration and astronomy, the two arts in which the Central and Southern American civilizations were pre-eminent, both with shamanistic overtones.

The Shaman as Benefactor

Of the mythologies more familiar to use, such as that of the Greeks, Prometheus bears most clearly the outlines of the shaman, especially as patron and benefactor of the human race.

As first created by the gods, humans were hardly more than animals. Prometheus took upon himself the task of elevating them and giving them sustenance. Having slaughtered and divided a bull, he made a smaller parcel of the edible portions which he wrapped up in the animal's stomach, while the bones and other parts he made into a larger one wrapped round with fat. Zeus, invited to pick which he wanted for himself, not unnaturally chose the bigger. Thus, sacrifice to the gods always consisted of the fat and bones of the animal while men and women ate the meat. Such was Zeus's anger at having been deceived that he denied humanity the gift of fire. Once more Prometheus came to the aid by stealing the fire of heaven.

These gifts were not the end to his benefactions. Like Quetzalcoatl, he taught the making of calendars so that men and women might know the seasons, gave them numbers, writing, farming, taught them to harness the horse, how to work metals, cure illness and prophesy.

All these things he did in the consciousness that they were contrary to the desires of the gods. Confronted with his deeds, his attitude was one of defiant challenge. According to Aeschylus, when Zeus condemned him to be bound by chains to a rock, his liver gnawed by birds, he hurled contempt in his teeth.

Prometheus is not, of course, himself a god but a Titan, a word which by etymology means 'over-reacher'. To overreach is to commit the worst of all sins, that of *hubris* or emulation of the gods, and the story of Prometheus was undoubtedly told as a cautionary tale of its dangers and of the innate human tendency towards it. Nevertheless, his true nature is never far from the surface. His chaining to the rock while the birds devour his entrails resembles the shaman's initiatory crisis which also involves the removal of viscera.

One of the shaman's commonest tasks is that of delivering his people from the thrall of a magical woman, a theme representing Prometheus's eternal combat with the female, here represented by Pandora. In this connection, one of the Titan's gifts, that of fire, is highly significant in that it releases man from his dependence on she who has been its sustainer and guardian hitherto.

And like the shaman, too, Prometheus is the trickster, acquiring by means of deception that which the inhabitants of the Other World do not wish to part with, but which is desirable for men and women.

In many of his characteristics Prometheus brings to mind Hercules who, of course, is not even a Titan, but a hero and may be based on an historical figure. There are, however, many contexts in which he seems to possess divine attributes and which involve the mastery of animals. In some he actually seems to be regarded as a god and this may arise from a somewhat surprising conflation. Diodorus of Sicily, among others, mentions a story in which Hercules, passing through Gaul, supposedly married the daughter of a tribal king who bore him a son called 'Galates', actually a synonym for 'Celts'.

Naturally, the proposition that the Celts owed their foundation to the Greek hero flies in the face of the evidence, so there must be another explanation. There is, in fact, a Celtic god who bears many of the attributes of Hercules including a cudgel. The name Ogmios by which he is frequently called is probably only one of several. Markale suggests he may also be In Dagda, the Good God, who, besides carrying a cudgel, has the same insatiability for food and sex as Hercules.

But, as we just saw, Kynon's black giant was also a cudgel-bearer and we have identified him with Cernunnos. So can Cernunnos be yet another *alter ego* of Ogmios? It seems to me probable. The famous Dorset hill-figure, the Cerne Abbas Giant, holds a cudgel in his right hand while his erect phallus suggests sexual virility. These would equate him with Ogmios-Dagda. But the name 'Cerne' contains a horn element, suggesting he is also Cernunnos.

Celtic tribes, and especially their royal families, usually claimed descent from gods, but so far as I am aware there was none in Gaul in which the names of Ogmios or Dagda occur. There are, on the other hand, several in which a form of 'horn', implying a descent from Cernunnos, figure.

The confusion now becomes explicable. A Greek traveller in Gaul, hearing of a Celtic tribe founded by a gluttonous and lecherous cudgel-carrying giant would conclude that he can only have been their own Hercules. That Diodorus makes reference to the story I take as confirmatory, for he was a supporter of Euhemerus's theory that those who came to be called gods were in origin heroes.

The Great Shaman

Though unarguably divine, another god who manifests the shamanic character of trickster is Odin. His designation as the Great Shaman has already been alluded to and, according to the descriptions we have of him, even his physical appearance suggests the magician. Portrayed as a vigorous man in his fifties, he wears a flowing cloak and a hat whose broad brim is intended to conceal the fact he has exchanged an eye for a single draught from the magic spring of Mimir which brought wisdom and understanding.

Like the shaman, he is a healer; like him, too, he possesses the gift of metamorphosis so that, as Snorri Storluson says, he could become a bird, a wild beast, a fish or a dragon. By his suspension from the World Tree, Yggdrasil, for nine days and nine nights, 'a sacrifice of myself to myself', he gained knowledge of the magic runes.

And in the story of his theft of the mead he shows himself most clearly in the guise of the shaman-trickster. During one of their rare periods of concord (so goes the myth) the two groups of gods, the Aesir and Vanir, created Kvasir, the all-wise. Unfortunately, he was killed by malign dwarves who then drained off his blood and mixed it with honey to make mead. Those that sipped it were inspired to write poetry and utter words of wisdom. However, the dwarves were themselves outwitted by the giant Suttung and his kin who snatched the mead from them.

Eager to regain it, the other gods assigned the mission to Odin. From the outset his chosen method was one of deception. First, he presented himself to the giant's mortal labourers, sharpening their scythes so effectively that they soon began to quarrel about possession of his magical whetstone and cut one another's throats. Odin then went to their employer and offered to take their place, asking only a sip of mead as the reward for his toil. The bargain was sealed but, when Odin had fulfilled his part of it, was treacherously withdrawn by Suttung.

His next stratagem was to bore a hole into the side of the mountain in which the giant lived. In the form of a serpent he inveigled himself through the small opening and successfully persuaded the giant's daughter to let him taste the mead. In

three gulps he drained the jars in which it was stored, took the
form of an eagle and flew back to Asgard, the home of the gods,
where he regurgitated it. In this way Odin became the god of
poetry, an art which is closely assimilated to shamanism.

As well as 'the intoxicator', by derivation the word 'mead' can
also mean 'the sweet' (because it was made from honey), or 'the
inspirer' and in this last interpretation has been used to associate
Odin with another form of inspiration. He himself, though not a
battle god, is the inspirer of martial qualities in men. In its
Germanic forms of Woden and Wotan, his name has been
connected with *Wut*, the warrior's battle-fury whose possible
connections with the shaman as master of fire have already been
noted.

Odin's famous eight-legged horse, Sleipnir, is also open to a
shamanistic interpretation. We have already seen that the drum
was often called the shaman's 'horse'. Some drums have four
thongs of leather stretched across the back to provide a hold for
the player's arm. Meeting at the centre, these would, of course,
make a web of eight strips. A Buryat story relates how a
shamaness's mare gave birth to an eight-legged foal. Believing
such a monster worthless, her husband hacked off four of them,
whereupon he was bitterly reproached because the eight-legged
foal was actually the physical incarnation of the one she rode in
her trance.

Another interpretation is that instead of a horse, Sleipnir is
actually a giant spider. Spiders of one sort and another are a
recurrent creature in shamanistic mythology, found in locations
as widely separated as Polynesia and Siberia. Some writers
believe that Ariadne who provided Theseus with the thread,
enabling him to escape from the Minotaur's lair after he had
killed it, was a spider. Arianrhod, the Other World girl who
appears in the Welsh story of *Math Son of Mathonwy* may well
have been another. Her name, which means 'Silver Wheel',
strongly suggests the spider's silvern web.

Ellis Davidson advances the proposition that the eight-legged
Sleipnir could be the bier on which a dead man is carried by its
bearers. If so, it would link Odin with his role as divine
psychopomp, also played by Mercury/Hermes, whose winged
helmet has earlier offered us a clue to his shamanic origin. He
was god of sleep and dreams, one of whose tasks was that of
closing the eyes of the dead. Hermes, too, is a trickster as when
he stole the cattle of Apollo, turning their shoes round so that
they would appear to have walked in the opposite direction.

Zeus, intending to reprove him, was instead won over by his charm and eloquence and made him his messenger. In another parallel with Odin, among areas assigned to Hermes was the promotion of commerce and the maintenance of the free rights of travellers on all the roads of the world.

He was also the inventor of certain minor forms of prophecy such as that involving knucklebones and was credited with the invention of the alphabet, of the musical scale and of astronomy.

Closely associated with Hermes is his half-brother Dionysus. As wine-giver, he was the god of the orgiastic Maenads, guilty among other outrages of tearing Orpheus to pieces. However, despite this instance of masculine-feminine religious antipathy, Dionysus also exhibits shamanistic traits which suggest a different, earlier epiphany and even in some comparatively late depictions, as for example on an ivory relief, he is shown as a horned god. The provenance of the relief is probably Orphic and in the Orphic Mysteries, Dionysus, the son of Zeus by Persephone, is the Suffering God. In other words, though probably formerly one and the same, the Orphic Dionysus is very different from that of the Maenads and there are a number of hints, besides the horns, that he may have been regarded as a Lord of the Animals.

Guthrie suggests that in his Orphic form he may have been an *alter ego* of Apollo, actually the god most venerated by the sect. Apollo is a solar deity and those most closely associated with shamanism invariably come into this category. As sun-god, he is *Phoibos*, the light bearer, but that light is as much metaphysical as literal; it is the light which, like that of Shamash, searches out truth or reveals the unseen future. As Alexikakos, he possesses the gift of healing.

Like another solar deity, the Celtic Belenos, he has an additional shamanistic quality: an association with water sources, such as the Castalian spring in which his priestesses, the Pythia, were required to take lustral baths before entering his Delphic sanctuary.

Though his twin sister, Artemis, was also Hecate, the patroness of witches, Apollo himself was vehemently antagonistic towards both witchcraft and everything feminine. His shrine at Delphi, like Yggdrasil, is a world-centre and a place of prophecy, though it is not only through the Pythia that Apollo prophesies, for he endows all his favourites with the gift. At the same time, we have the indisputable fact that he is the archer with the golden arrows, a metaphor for the shamanic trance still in use.

If we have no direct evidence of his being regarded as a Lord of the Animals and unlike Dionysus he never appears with horns, he is, nevertheless, associated with many different creatures. Like the Mesopotamian Shamash, he was once a shepherd and as such he is Nomios, protector of the flocks. As Apollo Smintheus, he is linked with mice; as Parnopius with locusts, as Lykoktonos with wolves. In this last form, some regard him as master of the wolves, that is to say able to guard the flocks from their depredations, while others believe he could transform himself into a wolf.

However, he is at his most shamanistic as the Apollo of the Hyperboreans. The Hyperboreans were a legendary people of superhuman gifts said to live idyllic, thousand-year lives in their land of perpetual snows beyond the North Wind, and it was to them that he repaired during his annual leave of absence from Delphi.

8. The Trance

Whatever power, privilege and prestige the shaman enjoys arises from his one unique and paramount gift: the ability to induce the trance through which he makes contact with the spirit world. He is a 'spirit-conjuror' in the strictest sense of the term and his imprint can be seen on all those other spirit-conjurors who crop up in history, from the black magicians of the Middle Ages to the magician Prospero in Shakespeare's *The Tempest* whom some believe to be based on the English magus John Dee and others on the Neapolitan Giordano Bruno.

None the less, the trance shows the same regional and other variations we have seen in all the manifestations of shamanism. In some places, for instance, the shaman is taken over by a spirit who uses him as a human mouthpiece. This has an obvious affinity to the trance-states of Spiritualist mediums. Elsewhere, the spirit does not in the strict sense 'possess' the shaman, but is 'summoned' into his presence. Usually invisible to all but the conjuror himself, it will declare its presence by making physical objects fly, causing drums to beat or trumpets to sound – again phenomena known to the seances of Spiritualism.

In other instances, though unseen to bystanders, it is believed to perch itself on the shaman's shoulder or the nape of his neck. According to contemporary accounts, this was said to be the way in which Apollo descended on the Pythia when they went into their oracular ecstasy. Such experiences could well be the basis for those stories from mediaeval times, where Satan was said to ride piggyback on witch or warlock or, as in the legend of St Christopher, where Christ manifests himself in a similar way. Examples of trances in which shaman and invoked spirit are as horse and rider are found all over the world and frequently equestrian terminology is used to describe it so that the shaman is said to be 'mounted' by the spirit.

Not all trance-states are so dramatic. A number of writers, including Backman and Hultkrantz, refer to what might be called a 'waking trance' in which the shaman appears to be behaving with complete normality, though he is in fact 'in touch' with his spirit-helper. This is used for what were regarded as comparatively minor activities such as healing and divination. The same authors quote from Tornaeus* who describes how a noiaidi, without the use of any aid, told him accurately all that had passed on his journey to the Lappmark.

However, the form of the trance most often regarded as characteristic and one quite distinct from those so far discussed, is that which entails what might be called a state of suspended animation for its duration. In the view of many authorities including Eliade, it is only where this is found that shamanism can be said to exist.

One is reminded of the stories brought home by travellers in India about the catalepsis induced by *fakirs* in which all the signs of life were temporarily suspended, but it is certainly not limited to the subcontinent, for descriptions coming from aboriginal Australia, North and South America and parts of Africa all testify to the universality of the practice. Backman and Hultkrantz's evidence includes the accounts of observers who visited Lappland when shamanism was still extant there, that is to say in the seventeenth and eighteenth centuries. Many of them formed the impression, though on how good a foundation it is impossible to know, that at the climax of his trance the shaman was to all appearances a corpse, even describing him as 'falling dead to the ground'. The language used by members of societies in which the shaman functions shows that he is indeed regarded by onlookers as in this condition. Thus, Norwegian Lapps spoke of the shaman 'lying dead while his spirit was wandering' and the Venezuelan Yaruro Indians of his body being 'a mere husk'. According to one of Backman and Hultkrantz's sources, the *Historia Norwegiae*, at least one shaman actually did die during the trance.

Trance-Induction

As I tried to make clear at the beginning of this book, a full shamanic seance is a very serious matter in which the entire community is deeply involved. The shaman will assiduously

* Tornaeus, Johannes, *Berattelse om Lapmarckerna och Deras Tillstand,* Svenska Landsmal XVII:3, Uppsala, 1900.

prepare for it through a period of abstention and purificatory rituals, the stringency of these depending on his objective and the degree of the spirit he wishes to contact. The more serious the former, the more exalted the latter or the heavier the demands he will be making of it, the greater the perils he puts himself in and, in consequence, the longer and more thorough the preparation. In such cases, at least for several days and sometimes for weeks, he will eat only lightly, if at all, and usually refrain from alcohol. That he will also eschew sexual intercourse and, in some instances, any contact with the opposite sex is only what one would expect.

Finally, on the day of the seance itself he will wash or bathe thoroughly, often in a special spring set apart for the purpose.

The basic method of trance-induction is through a combination of his song, his drumming and his dance. These, as we have seen, may be reinforced by breath-control techniques and, particularly, by the use of narcotics.

Some hold that the sheer physical effort of drum playing inhibits the onset of trance and in these cases, instead of being his own drummer, the shaman will leave it to an assistant or may have a group of percussionists present. The majority, on the other hand, seem to find the rhythmic arm, hand and finger movements helpful.

Although trances are said to have lasted as much as twenty-four hours or even longer, general observation assigns to them periods of from half an hour to about two hours. The signal for their ending is the shaman beginning to draw breath and then gradually stirring like a sleeper awakening from a particularly heavy slumber. Sometimes he will even go round greeting onlookers, shaking them by the hand, as if he has just returned from a long journey.

The duration of the trance as given by contemporary observers contrasts with descriptions by classical authors of what were undoubtedly shamanic journeys such as those of Aristeas of Proconnesus and Er the Pamphylian. Herodotus tells us, for instance, that among the earlier epiphanies of Pythagoras was as Hermotimus of Klazomenai, who may have lived in the eighth century BC. Hermotimus was given to 'rapts' in which he could leave his body to go in search of 'mantic knowledge', his quests apparently occupying him for years. His life ended when enemies, coming upon his inert physical remains, took it for dead and consigned it to the funeral pyre.

Journey to the Other World

If the disembodied voyager intends to visit the Other World – for he may, in fact, also travel invisibly in this one – his destination, can be either the Upper or the Lower World.

Some writers have concluded that the Upper World is the dwelling place of benevolent spirits and the Lower that of malevolent or, at any rate, harmful ones. Although such a belief is to be found in some areas, it is far from universal and, as we have seen, distinctions between abstract good and abstract evil play no significant part in shamnism. Consequently, where the distinction exists one is bound to supect that the instrusions come from outside. Certainly if one looks at shamanism from an historical perspective one finds little sign of any such polarity. Though those Celtic myths which have survived to our own times have undergone repeated redaction, it is plain that spirits from below the earth, and especially from beneath waters, are as benevolent as those whose dwelling is above. For example, Malory's King Arthur receives his sword from the hand of the Lady of the Lake, to whose keeping it is returned after his fatal wounding.

For all this, an Underworld which, like the Judeo-Christian Hell, is a place of evil and torment may have its roots in shamanism. According to early Hebrew belief, Hell was ruled over by the wicked Lilith, the mother of demons, and we have seen how frequently the notion of a powerful and dangerous woman occurs as queen of the Underworld.

Perhaps it is because it invariably involved a struggle between the male shaman and his ancient female enemy that Eliade declares the descent trance to be more dangerous than that of ascent. This he believes to be the reason why comparatively few accounts of them have been collected by European observers. None the less, he points out the descent is still undertaken as, for example, by Yakut shamans whose costume has a symbol representing an opening into the earth, while a linguistic distinction is drawn between the spirits above and those below.

The truth is, that as far as shamanism goes and despite a cloud of witness, even in the case of the upper realms it is not easy to piece together a coherent picture of the Other World which is free from self-contradictions.

Neither Castaneda, Harner nor any of the other writers who lay claim to direct experience is particularly helpful and in the end we are forced to rely on descriptions given to outsiders which we can surmise were intended to be taken metaphorically rather than literally. In many of them we have an ascent through seven (sometimes nine or fourteen) upper regions, obviously the prototypes of the Seven Heavens of Mesopotamia and the Seven Platonic Spheres. For some, these planes are the ascending branches of the World Tree, one of which contains the souls of those yet to be born and another those of future shamans. The attainment of the uppermost reaches will depend on ability or, in some cases, on the particular purpose of the shaman's seance, for it is not necessary always to scale the summit.

Although, on returning from his journey, the shaman will report his experiences to his audience, we have no detailed information about the nature of these spiritual landscapes. We do not, for example, have any description of the palace of Bai Uelgaen which is the destination of the Altaic shaman's ascent. It may, perhaps, be the case that, like those of the religious mystics, the experience is of such an ineffable character as to be incommunicable through the medium of words.

Ascent and Descent

When one sifts through the enormous body of information now available, the one clear point is that while experiences are regarded in some societies as characterizing the ascent-trance, in others they occur in those of descent. For example, among the Teleuts, the shaman may be waylaid on his upward journey by a woman who tempts him with food. If wise, he does not succumb, for the food, besides binding him to place, will also obliterate all memory of his past life.

The same motif is, of course, found in Greek myth as in that of Demeter, mother of Persephone, who is unable to liberate her daughter permanently from the Kingdom of Hades because she has imprudently eaten the seeds of the pomegranate.

Other World food or drink that expunges all memory of the past is another persistent shamanistic idea. Plato tells us that the soul, about to be reborn to a new earthly life after its sojourn in one of the Seven Spheres, must first drink from the Lethe, the Waters of Oblivion, so that all memory of this existence is lost. Only before the final reincarnation is the draught omitted and the entire cycle of previous lives, both earthly and heavenly, is remembered.

We have already noted how the motifs of the trance, such as the Narrow Bridge permeate literature and the same goes for the trance itself. The story of Rapunzel who allows her lover to use her dark tresses as a rope to climb to her high cell suggests the shamanic ascent, but there is an even clearer example in the English tale of Jack and the Beanstalk in which the hero actually wrests a succession of beneficial articles from a threatening being who lives in a castle at the top of the beanstalk. That he is a giant identifies him as an inhabitant of the Other World, for in all early representations of gods and mortals, the first are huge, and the second manikins, as, for instance, on the Gundestrupp Cauldron. Indeed, the convention of representing importance by stature survived well into the nineteenth century, as can be seen in numerous prints in which the size of the figures is in a strict proportion to position in the social scale.

The Jack of the beanstalk story is plainly the shaman-trickster, like Odin in the story of the recovery of the mead – also in the possession of a giant. In the Welsh story of *Kulhwch and Olwen* those who help to dupe the giant Ysbaddaden include Gwrhyr Interpreter of Tongues and Menw son of Teirwaedd, both, from the context, Druids.

The theme of descent occurs in Aladdin, taken by his magician uncle to the subterranean treasure cave. But it is evidence of the endurance of the idea that it can manifest itself even in the work of late writers quite unaware of the true significance of the images they were invoking, as in Lewis Carrol's *Alice in Wonderland*, and in Frances Hodgson Burnett's *The Secret Garden*.

In the graphic arts, as Michael Harner reminds us, representations of an opening into the Lower World consisting of a series of diminishing, concentric squares, like a perspective of arches, are found in the art of the Amerindians (in *The Way of the Shaman* he reproduces a drawing by a Hopi artist), as well as in many of the Tibetan *mandalas*.

Since the destination of the shaman's journey is a centre, the theme can be symbolized by labyrinths which, of course, always lead to a centre. These are found in mythology; for example, in that built by the craftsman-magician Daedalus for the Cretan Minotaur; and others have been uncovered by archaeology. An example of the latter is the kerbstone at the entrance to the passage graves at Newgrange in County Meath, Eire, on which labyrinth-patterns have been carved. (An interesting if late example is to be found in the nave of Chartres Cathedral. Here, the centre represents Jerusalem, the destination of pilgrimage, which is shown on some mediaeval maps as the centre of the world.)

According to Jungian psychologists, figures of this kind, and particularly the mandala, occur in the drawings of patients as they approach the successful climax of treatment, the so-called phase of 'individuation', further evidence of its penetration of the psyche.*

Images of Trance

What are we to make of the shaman's trance and, in particular, the claim that through it he actually separates spirit from body?

A decade or so ago, the response of most intelligent people to both would have been unequivocal. They belonged to the realms of dark ignorance and superstition. Admittedly at the time most of the available evidence was subjective: the descriptions given by shamans themselves to interrogators who, if sound academics, were, none the less, conditioned by the mores of Western, deterministic scepticism.

Now three developments have tended to make these attitudes less secure.

First, we have evidence of Western students undergoing shamanic training, such as those at Michael Harner's centre in Connecticut. Their witness, while still subjective, should be of a different order, for they are intelligent, articulate and presumably critical young people from our own culture.

In *The Way of the Shaman*, Dr Harner recounts the descriptions of some of those who, under his supervision, underwent the descent journey. The subject is asked to picture mentally some kind of entry into the earth, which may be a cave, the outlet of a rabbit's warren, even a manhole. A combination of drumming, a darkened room and relaxation is then employed to induce a light trance. In accounts they have given afterwards, some students have told how they found themselves going through the opening and descending a gradually sloping tunnel whose walls had a corrugated character, like a diminishing vista of arches. At first the tunnel is dark but, as a corner is turned, the light begins to increase. Finally, the subject will emerge into the open air. The scene that spreads before him or her, often described as like a particularly beautiful garden is, they aver, much more vivid than a dream location. The smell of flowers and earth will frequently be perceived, and they may even be aware of a soft breeze.

---

* Although the Jungian interpretation is somewhat broad and many of those so described are not strictly mandalas in the Eastern sense at all, the drawings of patients still exhibit what are often shamanistic motifs.

Such detailed descriptions are obviously impressive and might suggest new lines of investigation if it were not that the subjects are far from unanimous in their accounts of the experience. The impression gained in discussions with students who have participated in workshops of this kind is that these are the experiences of the few rather than the many, and that where they are actually said to have occurred they can be explained in ways that have nothing to do with shamanism.

It has also been pointed out that the images of trance are invariably derived from the subject's own culture. Just as the supernatural woman who figures in the dream of a devout Catholic will be described as the Blessed Virgin, so an Eskimo will encounter in his ecstasy those like himself.

Altered States of Consciousness

The second development in the conventional attitude is the recognition and study of so-called 'Altered States of Consciousness' which can occur in certain mental illnesses or may be induced; for example, by hypnosis or drugs. As anyone who has ever attended a jazz or rock concert will know, sustained, rhythmic drumming can have much the same sort of effect on some people, and it is not difficult to understand what can hapen when drumming is combined with the monotonous ullulation of the shaman's song and the physical sensations of his dance.

In *Divine Horsemen*, Maya Deren, a young American dancer, visiting Haiti on a Guggenheim scholarship, graphically describes the sensations produced in her by prolonged exposure to drum rhythms during a Voodoo rite she was attending. After a time she began to feel so taken over by the beat that it ceased to be outside, but actually within her own body as physical reponses of foot tapping and clapping becoming as involuntary as muscular spasms beyond her control. At the climax she lapsed into a kind of coma which she described as like being engulfed 'in bright darkness'. She was later told she had spoken with the voice and vocabulary of a deity whom those around her identified as the love-goddess Erzulie.

From examples of this kind, it is clear why the drum is given such an important place in shamanism at large.

As to the neurophysiological mechanism involved, it is known that certain drugs which depress metabolic reactions and so effect the functioning of the autonomic nervous system can produce similar symptoms to those described by Maya Deren. In her case and in shamanic drumming the stimulus may be a combination of the regular rhythm patterns with the auditory frequencies of the drum itself.

The Paranormal

However, perhaps the most interesting evidence comes from the third of the three developments mentioned. This is the growth of new attitudes towards psychic and paranormal phenomena and, with it, a marked willingness to investigate them dispassionately.

One which has preoccupied researchers is what has come to be called 'out-of-the-body' experience in which, as the phrase implies, the subject believes he has left his own body and in his incorporeal state is able to wander at will. One of the first to make a public statement on the subject was the English novelist William Gerhardi who, in *Resurrection,* claimed to have verified the reality of his absences from the physical through the cooperation of his wife. He was able to describe to her alterations in the layout of objects perceived during disembodied wanderings round the house but which she alone knew of and which had been returned to their normal places before he had a chance to see them.

However, even before Gerhardi, two Americans, Sylvan Muldoon and Hereward Carrington were investigating the subject and published their findings in 1929 in *The Projection of the Astral Body,* based on experiences the former had been having from his late teens. After publication of the first and then a second book, they were inundated with thousands of descriptions from readers who had had similar experiences. Many of these were incorporated into later works.

There are in all of them, as recorded, factors common not only to each other, but also to shamanic trance. To begin with, none of the subjects was in a normal state of consciousnes, but were in states varying from slight drowsiness to the deep coma of grave illness. Suddenly and often to their intense surprise, though none reports any sense of fear, they would realize that, though in a familiar environment, they were viewing it from an unaccustomed perspective.

The witnesses represent a broad cross-section. Very few had previously had any belief or interest in psychical or paranormal research or were members of or sympathizers with any occult movement. Many had never heard of the phenomenon before it occurred; some had hitherto kept the experience secret out of the fear that doubt might be cast on their sanity.

One typical woman witness tells how, while idly reading a book, she suddenly realized its print had grown small. She then saw she was looking down on it from a position high overhead, and near the ceiling. Immediately afterwards she saw her own body seated in a chair, the book open on her lap.

In a minority of cases we have additional information: the subjects claim to have travelled great distances in their disembodied state, even visiting friends who have later testified to the visitation and who, at the time, took the shades for the physical presence. Thus, one American woman, a Doctor of Philosophy working as a professor of English at a mid-western university, records going from a New York hospital to the home of an artist acquaintance in Los Angeles.

An even smaller minority, which includes Muldoon himself, add a yet more bizarre detail. They report being in the presence of spirits. In one case a man, while having a tooth extracted in a situation which, because of complications, required a general anaesthetic, found himself in a transparent-walled room through which he could see all that was happening to him while a woman, in nun's habit, engaged him in conversation as he watched.

As is always the case, whether one finds the accounts convincing will depend on subjective factors, but there is a second and perhaps surprising source of them. Although Muldoon and Carrington describe many instances which occurred during illness, after an accident and when death seems imminent, it is perhaps surprising to find the medical profession actually producing confirmatory evidence, independently and often in apparent ignorance of the American and other studies.

The subjects here are most frequently those in intensive care who will evince all the symptoms of death. The complex and sophisticated techniques of resuscitation will at once be set in motion. Where these are successful, the patients will frequently describe after recovery how they watched like spectators while the drama centering upon their own bodies was acted out. In some instances they have been able to provide collateral detail of the scene.

Such is the volume of these accounts that a word, 'autoscopy', or self-seeing, has been coined to describe it.

At the same time, exhaustive scientific studies of the 'out-of-body' experience are being conducted by Dr Susan Blackmore at the Brain and Perception Unit at Bristol University and, under Dr Celia Green, at the Institute for

Psychophysical Research at Oxford. Both have written books about their researches, increasing understanding of the subject, knowledge of which is constantly being supplemented as fresh data becomes available.

PART IV: THE SHAMAN AND HIS INFLUENCE

9. Eclipse and Revival

As we have seen, shamanism, masculine and with its origins in the hunting phase, exists largely in a state of perpetual feud with the beliefs and practices inaugurated by the feminine growers. Yet if one looks at world religions past and present one cannot fail to be struck by a paradox: while all incorporate elements drawn in roughly equal proportions from both, they are, without exception, male dominated. For example, although the Egyptians were agriculturists and it is plain that much in their religion derives from an archaic Earth Mother cult, actual worship was firmly in the hands of a male priesthood.

The Blessed Virgin Mary has frequently been likened to an Earth Mother, a similarity heightened when one realizes that many of the terms used in the Litanies of Mary were taken verbatim from those addressed to Isis during the period of her maximum popularity in pagan Rome. Equally, the central sacrifice of Christianity – the slaying and burial in the earth of a young man – obviously evokes echoes of those sacrifices involving the vegetation god.

Yet as a religion Christianity is male dominated.

At the same time, we have to admit that even on the most cursory inspection, the dominant males in both the Egyptian cult of Isis and in Christianity are not at all like shamans. They are, of course, priests and as Campbell points out, the priest is something quite different. Indeed, by Dioszegi's definition, he is automatically excluded from the category, since the priestly apprenticeship involves deliberate study and requires of him no personal crisis. Furthermore, he lays claim to no unique, divinely granted gifts and, where the shaman is concerned with the specific human crisis, the priest regards all the crises of life as the result of lapses in the application of an immutable, divinely ordained code.

In view of the priest's supremacy in formalized religion, we have to conclude that by the time we encounter it, both the women of the Earth Mother cults and the shamans have been supplanted.

How and why did this come about?

We have already mentioned the Apache Hactcin. The legends of the Apache tell how shamans began to appear on earth and were soon quarrelling about which of them was the most powerful. The exasperated Hactcin caused an eclipse of sun and moon, then challenged the shamans to bring them back. Despite the most spectacular displays of magic, none succeeded and, at last, the Hactcin themselves had to do so. This was not the end of their interventions for, at the same time, they also created thunder, rain and the rainbow, and divided the seasons. They then chose the twelve most skilled of the shamans and split them into two groups, one to represent summer, the other winter, and gave them the name of Tsanati. It was at this time that the Hactcin also planted the first seeds, thus inaugurating agriculture.

The story is told as the origin of the Tsanati dance society of the Jicarilla Apache. The dance society, which institutionalizes what had hitherto been a spontaneous activity, is not infrequently a step in the progression to religion. Taking it in conjunction with the first seed-planting, Campbell interprets the whole myth as a symbolical account of the way in which shamanism, with its elitist individualism, was superseded by the group-oriented practices of the seed-planters. Thus, the Tsanati of the Hactcin's creation are less shamans than priests.

He sees the narrative as the counterpart to those in the mythologies of the Hindus, Persians, Greeks, Celts and Germans, in which Titans are vanquished by gods. The Titans are the shamans; the gods those of institutional religion, and their functionaries, like the Tsanati, are the priests. And the process whereby the priest displaces the shaman is simultaneously the one in which, on Campbell's thesis, a society without structure is replaced by a structured, agriculturalist one.

The argument is one I find a little hard to accept. For one thing, by no means all the Titans of world myth have any hint of the magical about them. For another their destruction, where it does occur, is frequently encompassed by beings themselves markedly shamanistic. The shamans of the Orphic Rhapsodies are not the Titans but those who overcome the Titans' machinations and restore the Suffering God.

More importantly, while it is undoubtedly true that agriculture calls for the degree of organized cooperation, implying an ordered society, such qualities are not necessarily missing from the hunt. Certainly if one looks at the cave drawings, the impression one gets is of organized cooperative effort. We also know from studies of nomadic peoples that their social organization is such as to be almost military. Just as, living in the confined space of the yurt, everything had to have its assigned place, so every able-bodied member of the tribe had his tasks, which besides encompassing those necessary to the economy, also included defence against natural as well as human enemies.

Finally, what Campbell's interpretation of the Apache story fails to explain is why institutionalized religion should have become, without exception, a male province. I believe we may have clearer signposts to what happened in another universal theme: that of the mating of Sky God and Earth Mother.

As we saw in Chapter 6, the former is as intimately bound up with the beliefs of the shaman as the latter is with those of agriculturist. On a superficial view, therefore, their union might seem to be the achievement of concord between the sexes. In fact, it is nothing of the kind. Their mating is not the consummation of a partnership; it is the overcoming of the one by the other, the submission of feminine to masculine through which the queen-sovereign becomes the queen-consort. It is the same dethronement as that in the account of how the Greeks' veneration of the Sky God, Apollo, replaced that of the Earth Mother, Gaia, a change dated to about the middle of the second millennium BC.

I believe this and all similar stories to mark the same discovery: that of the male role in conception. It was one by which the ancient, terrifying power of the female was nullified. And the whoop of male triumph resounds down the millennia. In his own eyes at least, he is installed in the seat of authority. The reversal which has taken place in the attitudes of the sexes is well illustrated in the *Oresteia* cycle of Aeschylus. In the final play of the trilogy, *The Eumenides*, Orestes is arraigned before the gods for the murder of his mother in revenge for her slaughter of his father, Agammemnon. The verdict rests on the question of whether it is more heinous to kill father or mother. The divine judges rule in favour of the former since the male is the provider of the seed; the woman the mere soil in which it is planted.

However, there was a second and equally important aspect to the discovery. Once made, the male felt himself to have been the gull of a gross and protracted confidence trick. Women had deceived men about the part they had always been playing in bringing about new life. They were the witches, the Great Deceivers. 'Keep women under rule', admonished one of the aphorisms adorning the walls of Apollo's Delphic shrine.

And 'kept under rule' they were. Heroic women figures abound in Greek myth and drama from Athena as the warrior-woman to Antigone prepared to embrace a miserable death immured in a cave rather than allow the body of her brother Polynices to be deprived of its funeral rites. Nevertheless, in life as opposed to literature the role of women was undoubtedly a secondary one. They were given only a rudimentary education, if any at all; when their husbands entertained they were expected to cook the meal but otherwise to remain out of sight.

And what is true of Greece was true for almost every society – and has remained so.

The Growth of the City

Myths can frequently be interpreted on more than one level and that of the union of Earth Mother and Sky God not only marks the recognition of the male role, but, in my view, a watershed no less momentous.

In general, providing it is sufficiently fertile and they are not driven off it by enemies or some other catastrophe, the grower remains fixed to the land he cultivates – that is why we speak of 'sedentary agriculture'. By contrast, the hunter in his search for quarry and the nomad in his for grazing is compelled to move ever further afield. Sooner or later, these migrations will bring them to places already inhabited, often by the agriculturists. Thus are the people of the Sky God brought into collision with those of the Earth Mother.

History and pre-history abounds with cases. It was in this way that one confederation of Indo-European tribes, the Greeks, having overrun the peninsula bounded by the Mediterranean, the Adriatic and Aegean, found themselves in territories occupied by the agriculturist Pelasgians.

Wherever the encounter took place, two results flowed from it.

Now in the incipiently hostile environment of those on whose lands they had disposed themselves, the newcomers were forced to build protective pallisades. Thus, the city, one of humanity's greatest and most successful steps not only in adapting to, but in shaping its environment, came into being, like so many others, as a by-product, in this case of the need of invaders to make themselves secure. It has continued to be so. Whether in Sumer in the Third and Fourth Millennia BC, in mediaeval Europe or in the Americas when Europeans began colonizing them, one unfailingly finds the invader and his defensive perimeter, the embryo of the walled cities.

Circumscribed by these very walls were the old religious practices which, hitherto, had taken place in the depths of the countryside. Now they have to be brought within the safety of the city's purlieus. The temple came into existence, its past among the trees of the sacred grove recalled by its columns, integral to religious architecture, but whose origins are demonstrated in many striking examples. One is to be found in the twelfth-century Abbey Church of Notre Dame at Beaugency-sur-Loire. Here, at the end of a wide nave, twelve columns are so grouped as to form an almost complete circle – a sacred grove wrought in stone. And to underline the point, at its epicentre stands a font, a place of initiation.

Replacement of Local Gods

But there was another effect. What particularly distinguishes city life from that of the village is, more than anything else, a high degree of cooperation and interdependence, typified by its communal services and divisions of labour. Although nomadic existence might partly have prepared the colonists for the new life, what it had not prepared them for was a difference in scale. In the old homelands everyone knew everyone else. This included the ruler who, now in his palace, was invisible at the very time when the enormously increased complexity of existence was calling for visible, authoritative and, as compared with the old way, even oppressive rule.

And if it was important for him to persuade his own people of his unquestionable dominance, it was vital to convince the subjugated that, alien though they might be, he and his people were unassailable.

At the same time, for the nomads, consolidating themselves in their new homeland, there was another consideration. It must soon have become obvious that agriculture as they saw it being practised by the autochthonous population was an extremely reliable means of obtaining food. They would have begun to emulate them – and therefore needed the blessing of the agriculturists' gods.

The only answer to all these problems was for the ruler to make it clear that he himself enjoyed unlimited divine patronage, not only that of the gods of his tribe, but of the gods of the occupied as well. He appointed himself their earthly vicar.

Establishing his mastery of the local gods is everywhere one of the first acts of the conqueror. The invading Romans – the first British city-builders as the suffix '-chester' in so many placenames recalls – had no sooner landed than the Druidic groves rang with their axes, the sacred timber providing material for temples dedicated to their own gods.

To complete the supersession, the deities of the original inhabitants were equated with those of the newcomers. The Celtic Belenos becomes the Graeco-Roman Apollo; the Great Goddess of the Pelasgians receives her Hellenized name Demeter, which actually means 'Earth Mother'.

And here we have the second interpretation of the myth of the union of Sky God and Earth Mother. It symbolizes the gods of the invaders overwhelming those of the invaded.

The Fate of the Shaman
And what we have as a result is exactly the severely masculine religious environment typical of most of the civilizations known to us from the past.

Totally banished are the women of the old religious practices, surviving only as the 'wise women', which is exactly what the word 'witch' means, practising their craft in secrecy, the fierce barbarity of their repression a measure of the awe which still clung to them.

But what became of the other mediators, the shamans? In some places they survived, becoming not only king-makers, but also king-slayers for, in his new role, the temporal ruler might himself have to become the chosen mate of the fertility goddess. In others, they were demoted to royal advisers on auguries and portents. In still others they were banished as ruthlessly as the women.

The first happened in that province where ritual regicide was practised, an area which included a large swathe of Africa and India, as well as the Celtic lands. Elsewhere, as in Mesopotamia, we find priesthoods whose reputation as magicians betrays their shamanistic past.

In Greece, as in Rome, the tribal shaman was totally banished.

The Revival of the Shaman

However, despite proscription, though they faded away, they did not die. In the form of Dodds's 'Greek shamans' they were to return.

Their resurgence in socio-economic milieux so unlike the original – a phenomenon which occurred not once but repeatedly – raises new and intriguing questions. For if shamanism properly belongs to a remote and archaic past, its revival even in modified form is as incomprehensible as if we ourselves reverted to feudalism, disposing ourselves in a hierarchy of fiefs owing allegiance to a king and with serfs and villeins under a liege-lord.

In his *Ecstatic Religion*, Ioan Lewis tries to show that such regressions are the compensatory device of the deprived and, to be sure, in many of the cases he cites, such as the slave-religions and snake-handling sects of North America, he is no doubt right. The popularity among women of the cult of Dionysus can partly be explained as redressing the humiliatingly subsidiary role to which their sex was relegated in Greek life. However, the fact is that it, like the slave and the snake-handling religions, all belong more properly not in the category of shamanism but in that of the vegetation cults, in which ecstasy, *entheoi*, is available to all.

By contrast, the revival of shamanistic ideas can be seen to occur among those who were not the least deprived but from an affluent, educated middle class. As Ioan Lewis himself agrees, Dionysus moved among all classes; Apollo was found 'only in the best society'.

The real answer must lie elsewhere.

From about the sixth century BC the orthodox religious ideas of the Greeks were being exposed to radical criticism. Though the traditional festivals and sacrifices were observed, its practices were seen as becoming increasingly ossified, and its mythology continued to represent humans as the mere playthings of capricious and unpitying deities.

The period saw the popularization of the Mystery religions, among them that founded by an eighth-century Thracian, Orpheus, known to us from his journey into the Underworld to rescue his dead wife, Eurydike, a journey immediately suggesting the shaman. In fact, he was probably one of those hashish-smoking Thracian mystics called *kapnobatai*. He was also a religious reformer, advocating especially the worship of 'the most shamanistic of the gods', venerated in the most shamanistic of all his guises: as the Apollo of the Hyperboreans.

Orphism had obvious merits. Apart from its scripture in the form of the 'Orphic Rhapsodies', it had a creed which included a kind of rudimentary doctrine of original sin and a belief in reincarnation. The individual, though involved in an unending struggle between the unruly titanic and the divine aspects of his nature, could hope that he would be requited in some future life for present distresses.

But, as was typical of the Apolline cults, these benefits were available only to men. No woman was ever initiated.

One of the most eminent Orphics was the sixth-century philosopher-mystic Pythagoras. The name 'Pythagoras' actually means 'Mouthpiece of Apollo' and throughout his life he was so closely linked with the god that some actually spoke of him as his son or his incarnation. He even possessed the physical sign-manual which, traditionally, the spirits placed on those they have chosen to be shamans. It took the form of his famous 'golden thigh', gold being the colour of Apollo, and was probably a birthmark.*

In middle life Pythagoras travelled to Crete, home of the purest form of Orphism and there underwent an initiation which involved spending days and nights alone in one of the caves on Mount Ida. It was followed by a rite in which his own death and rebirth was mystically enacted. The mind leaps back to the Eskimo shaman and to the Australian Aranda mentioned in Chapter 3.

Thereafter, he went on to Egypt, probably Persia – home of the Magi – and, if we believe some witnesses – Babylon. It is not difficult to understand why he chose to visit one or both places. Despite Biblical denunciations of them as 'magicians, seers and exorcists', the Mesopotamian priesthoods, like the Persian Magi were extraordinarily gifted men responsible for an upsurge of knowledge such as the world has never since seen and much of which is still with us. It is to them that we owe all our measurements of time, for it was they who divided the circle into 360 degrees of angle. Applied to the motions of the heavenly bodies, it made it possible to divide the year into twelve, roughly equal, segments.

As evidence that Pythagoras was influenced by them we have the notorious theorem once attributed to him, but now known to

---

* For a more detailed description of his life, times and ideas see Ward Rutherford, *Pythagoras: Lover of Wisdom*, Aquarian Press, 1984.

have been familiar enough to the Babylonians for them to teach it to their young. We may also recall that, like the Babylonians, he was an astronomer responsible, among other things, for the theory of the Harmony of the Spheres.

However, the classification of phenomena into 'natural' and 'supernatural' was one as unknown to the Mesopotamians as it was to the Greeks. All science had a magical purpose and knowledge – *philosophia* – was first and foremost knowledge of the divine plan and hence, for the individual, a means of overcoming the titanic.

If esoteric wisdom was Pythagoras's objective he seems to have been successful. In his own lifetime he was credited with such miraculous abilities that he was designated a 'daimon', that is to say, a being midway between mortal and god. He could heal the sick; like Orpheus he was a musician who could charm all animal creation with his song. Most significantly he was able to visit the spirit world in trance.

Returning to Greece, Pythagoras left his native island of Samos, and went to Croton on the boot of Italy and then part of Greater Greece where he established a community of followers.

The Pythagoreans were antifeminist and, in particular, terrified of witches and their spells. Apuleius makes clear in the *The Golden Ass* exactly what can happen to those whose misfortune or imprudence lands them in their clutches.

The Croton community may have survived its founder, who is said to have died during a populist uprising against it. Finally dispersed during the early fifth century, the Pythagoreans set up new communities at Thebes on the Greek mainland and in the Peloponnese.

It was here that Socrates encountered and was influenced by them. According to his disciple, Plato, the sage was himself given to falling into trances. In *The Phaedo* he gives at least oblique hints of his belief in a form in which it was possible to leave the body, and implies that, if not already part of the mental equipment of the philosopher, it was something he should cultivate.

Science and the Shaman

That ferment which had shaken sixth-century Greek intellectual life was repeated as the Roman Empire was undergoing its death-pangs.

Like the British later, the Romans had seen imperial expansion and the bringing of civilization to barbarians as a divinely ordained mission. When the empire was forced to retrench the myth was demolished, impelling the quest for another. Among a plethora of manifestations was the revival of the teachings of Pythagoras by Apollonius of Tyana and their gradual merging with Platonism in the highly esoteric form of Neoplatonism.

The next great period of intellectual and, in particular, religious upheaval was in fifteenth-century Europe. Here the impetus was twofold: the spread of the Protestant reform movement and the new Copernican astronomy which, by exchanging the sun for the earth as the centre of the universe, at once cast doubt on scripture and demoted the habitat of humanity. As a way out of the new impasse and to try to reconcile the new ideas with those of the past, men and women began looking to classical learning and, among other directions, toward Pythagoreanism and Neoplatonism.

At the same time, as a means of trying to discover the Divine Will, which at that time must have seemed so opaque, they experimented in magic. The Neapolitan magus, Giordano Bruno cultivated a 'Gnostic trance', in which, as in the shamanic, it was supposed to be possible to liberate the soul from the body, though his success is unrecorded. In Britain, John Dee, a man of enormous learning and breadth of scholarship, employed a medium, Kelley, to help him contact the world of celestial spirits.

The activities of the Renaissance mages proved impotent to prevent the convulsions of the Reformation and, at its end, the magical and shamanistic was suppressed as ruthlessly by the new as it had been by the old Church.

Almost two centuries elapsed before the throwing down of a fresh challenge – one to rock the edifice of faith more deeply than Copernicus, Galileo or Luther had done. It was, of course, the publication of Charles Darwin's *The Origin of Species*. If heliocentric astronomy had displaced the earth, now it was the turn of the human species itself. Instead of being the offspring of a single, God-created couple ordained to occupy the supreme position in Creation, they were no more than another species of mammal, unique in some of their capacities, but caught up in the same 'struggle for existence' as the rest.

As a world best seller, *The Origin of Species* was to be more influential on every facet of thought, including the political, than anything since the Gospels themselves and, just as earlier epochs had seen the emergence of Orphism, of Pythagoreanism, of Neoplatonism, of Renaissance magianism, our own was to witness something similar.

The beginnings of the Spiritualist movement are usually traced to 1848 and the famous incident of the Hydesville Ghost in New York when the two Fox sisters, Margaret and Kate, devised a code in which they could reply to the rappings of what was taken to be a ghost. There was, in fact, nothing particularly original in their act and undoubtedly the recording of the Hydesville Ghost in the history books came about partly because of the considerable business acumen of the two girls' elder sister, who soon had them giving public lectures and displays. But there can surely be little doubt that its principal cause was the climate of the times: the Darwinian revolution and the search for new mythologies it had sparked.

It is scarcely necessary to enumerate the many parallels between Spiritualism and shamanism, of which the most striking is obviously the common belief in spirit worlds and the ability of humans to make contact with them in altered states of consciousness. But there are others: the belief in the Seven Spheres of Existence, for example, the considerable emphasis laid on healing, belief in the tripartite division of the human personality and, in many cases, in reincarnation.

These characteristics are even more pronounced in Theosophy. Helena Blavatsky, its founder, had originally been associated with Spiritualism, but, because of disagreement on a number of points, broke away to found her own organization. To the existing credo of the Spiritualists and its preoccupation with paranormal phenomena was added, in particular, the belief in an Ancient Wisdom given to humanity by a root-race which, in due course, left the mortal plane to become discarnate masters, continuing thereby to exert their benign influence – overtones of the Hyperboreans and the Hesiodic Golden Age.

Theosophy itself, while still in existence, is to some extent rivalled by other groups. One was Anthroposophy, founded by the Austrian Rudolf Steiner, originally a Theosophist. Steiner traced the beginnings of his interest in the subject to the scientific writings of the German Goethe, author of *Faust*, whose own inquiries took him into realms very like those inhabited by the Renaissance mages.

Steiner's Anthroposophy has in many ways been the most profoundly influential of all these movements, especially in its advocacy of 'biodynamic' methods of farming and in education where the Rudolf Steiner or 'Waldorf' schools have provided an alternative to what was otherwise available in Britain and in Continental Europe. None the less, its beliefs echo those of Theosophy, and hence of shamanism in many ways, in particular in its belief in reincarnation and in an original Ancient Wisdom.

Though it would be manifestly absurd to pretend that the shamanistic is ever totally absent from human life, the evidence certainly suggests that it expands from an eclectic into a popular movement at those moments when the accepted image of the universe and our own destiny in it are most under criticism.

Whether this vitiates its ideas is, of course, another question and one we shall have to examine later.

10. Was Shamanism a Universal Religion?

In the course of this book we have come upon many striking affinities in the shamanistic practice of geographically separated peoples. These have, of course, been noted by others and explained in many different ways. For instance, to traditional anthropology, they are the ubiquitous response of 'primitive' minds to such great natural mysteries as death. In Frazer's famous dictum they are 'the effect of similar causes acting on the similar constitution of the human mind in different countries and under different skies'.

Though spontaneous development must frequently have taken place, it can hardly be taken as the sole explanation, for what natural progression of logic leads to the hypothesis that death was due to ejection of a spirit? The concept of spirit is, in itself, one so sophisticated that it is surely expecting a lot of the 'similar constitution of the human mind' that it should have occurred to it universally?

To others, manifestations like shamanism are the accompaniment of particular evolutionary phases, in this case that of tribal hunting and pastoralism, so it is a purely socio-economic phenomenon.

The test of every hypothesis is, not only whether it can account adequately for the phenomenon under consideration, but whether it can be used as an instrument of prognostication. Hence, if this were true we should be able to predicate the existence of shamans in every tribal hunting or nomadic society. And so far so good. As far as I am aware, no society at these stages which did not have something equivalent has ever been encountered.

What is more, those which, for one reason or another, return to these forms of economy will usually also revert to a form of shamanism. African Negroes were taken to the Caribbean to work as slaves on the British sugar-plantations. After their emancipation, groups of them formed small, isolated fishing communities. At the same time, they borrowed from the neighbours, the native Caribs, the *obeah*, a wise man fulfilling many of the functions of the shaman.

In other cases, as we shall see in the next chapter, shamanism may be disguised under an appearance of Christianity or one of the other major religions.

There is, however, another prediction we should be able to make: we would expect to find shamanism replaced by something quite different as the economic structures of a society themselves changed. But here, as the previous chapter showed, there is less than unanimity. In some circumstances shamanism is capable of surviving such changes, though it may adapt its forms. An example repeatedly encountered has been Celtic society. It was tribal; in the past, it had survived on hunting and pastoralism. It therefore fulfilled the criteria of a society in which one would expect to find shamanism and so we do – in the form of Druidism. Yet by Caesar's time, when the Celts were practising sedentary agriculture, the Druids had lost none of their powers. If anything they had actually increased them.

Again, as we saw in the last chapter, even when far more profound changes took place, such as with the foundation of cities, the shaman, though transformed into priestly magician often wielded considerable authority.

But there are other factors of which the socio-economic theory fails to give account. For example, while one can accept that similar basic patterns could emerge under similar structures, it is testing credulity to believe that it could produce the detailed correspondences we have found, for example, in the persistence of such motifs as the Sky Spirit, the Narrow Bridge or the Great Centre.

Another explanation might be ethnic origin. That the Tibetans and Hopi Indians of Arizona both use the same image to represent the forms of the tunnel down which the shaman makes his descent could be because both come from the same Mongolian racial stock. If the tunnel image were limited to ethnically related peoples one might be forced to agree, but they also occur in the fantasy drawings of European and American psychiatric patients. And almost all the similarities we have noted can be found among peoples for whom there is no trace even of contact, let alone common origin, as, for instance, the

Siberians and the Australian aborigines or the Celts and pre-Columbian civilizations of Latin America.

This particular difficulty is overcome in another hypothesis. Some psychologists, and perhaps notably orthodox Freudians, might contend that the reason why images such as the mandala are found in so many, widely scattered environments is, quite simply, because they stand for that which is indisputably universal: the vagina. The shaman's descent thus becomes a *regresso in utero*, the fantasy re-enactment of the unconscious desire by which the male in particular is supposed to be haunted throughout life, that of return to the womb. Evidence of this is to be found in our tendency to assume the foetal position in sleep or by the gratification most of us obtain from steeping in hot bath, a requickening of the buried memory of the intrauterine fluid. Even sexual intercourse itself may, it has been suggested, represent the desire on the part of the male to re-enter the womb.

Pursuing the same argument, the beautiful landscapes described by some of Michael Harner's students as opening up when they reached the nadir of their descent, could be taken as the symbolic depiction of that idyllic, pre-natal existence when every need was met automatically and without effort. It is far from coincidental that water – the amniotic fluid – in the form of fountains or ornamental pools is a common feature of these scenes.

And have we not already noticed how the burial mounds replicate the female sexual organs and how the shaman's Lower World is itself frequently associated with a female?

The psychoanalytical theory can also, of course, be applied to the ascent-trance. Freud's Tenth Lecture in *A General Introduction to Psychoanalysis* is devoted to the symbols adopted by the unconscious mind. As is now well known, he sees those of ascent, among which he specifically mentions poles and trees, as phallic. So, by extension, are those of flying, including ones in which the dreamer himself flies.

In view of the uncompromisingly masculine cast of shamanism, the incidence of that which stands so unambiguously for the male is wholly consistent. Indeed, phallism actually plays a central part in the Bon religion of Tibet, as well as in Taoism and Tantrism.

Nevertheless, persuasive as it may seem superficially, the Freudian explanation, too, is fraught with weaknesses. According to accepted dogma, the use of symbols as euphemisms for certain bodily parts came about because, to the nineteenth century, they were regarded as subjects unfit even to be thought about, let alone openly discussed. Symbols were the subterfuge of the lustful libido to circumvent these constraints. But if these mental evasions are due to prudery, it is a little hard to see why societies in which it was absent should have been under the necessity of indulging in them. They not only could, but plainly did, call a spade a spade.

It might also be pointed out that there are, in any case, more obvious explanations for some of these typical images of shamanism. Since most of the substances used for trance-induction produce a sensation of flying, it is scarcely surprising if flight metaphor occurs in its language. The same goes for the ascent symbols such as the ladder or the notched stake which stands both for the shaman's spiritual ascent and for the Great Centre which is his destination.

A Unitary System?

What we seem to be left with is the proposition that, because of their many detail similarities, at some point in distant prehistory all the various existing species of shamanism must have formed part of a unitary system. That is to say that shamanism occurred in one place and spread thence outward. Put another way, shamanism as found today is the corrupt remnant of what had once, in some lost, primeval epoch, been a world-wide system of belief.

At once many mysteries are elucidated, not only the detail of the similarities, but why, for example, those shamans with whom contemporary observers have come into contact invariably insist they are but the feeble heirs of men of infinitely greater gifts and powers. The idea also accords with the views of those who subscribe to the theory of an Ancient Wisdom and its masters or in such of its permutations as that in which a repository of knowledge is said to have been transmitted to humanity by well-disposed extraterrestrial visitants who perpetually monitor our activities from their UFOs.

Although outside of Hesiod's 'Golden Age' and the apocryphal Hyperboreans, there is no evidence whatsoever for either the discarnate Masters or the extraterrestrials, the single-source theory is not inherently untenable. We now know that there was far more trade over far greater distances than was formerly believed and that it began much earlier. In Brighton Museum is a cup, in every respect like those in use today but dated to the Third Millennium BC. It is made from Baltic amber, suggesting that it was the result of trade between people living on what is now the Sussex coast and those living in the far north of Europe. There are other examples. From very early times, Chinese merchants were using not only the famous Silk Road for moving goods, but also sea routes which took them into the Mediterranean, while artefacts have been found in Brazil marked with Phoenician script.

That trade is an important medium for the transmission of ideas is demonstrated by the Phoenicians themselves. Among those they passed on was their alphabet, the basis of those of Hebrew and Greek and so, indirectly, our own.

Nevertheless, the obstacles in the way of acceptance remain formidable. First, there is the demonstrable fact that shamanism can and does occur spontaneously, given the appropriate circumstances. Secondly, it goes back much further even than the Third Millennium and it is hard to see what routes of transmission could have been available as early as 30,000 BC and what was being traded.

But could it not be the case that it began so early as actually to predate the diffusion of the human race over the earth? That is to say it came into being at a time when the first group of humanoids were huddled together round a single hearth and was diffused as this primary group itself spread. Perhaps. But can we really believe that the kind of concepts we have come across belong to or would be relevant to so early a phase?

The Diffusion of Shamanism

We are left, finally, with an explanation which to some extent synthesizes others. According to this, core shamanism may have arisen spontaneously, but evolved in different directions in different regions.

Given the premise, it is not difficult to imagine that in some remote, landlocked corner of the globe, a group of shamans, perhaps those of neighbouring tribes, decided to sacrifice some of their characteristic individualism to federate themselves in a single body. Thus united, their basic lore could have been built up into a coherent system, something nearer to what we should recognize as a philosophy, while the horizons of practical knowledge, such things as herb-medicine and astronomy, could have been dramatically advanced.

In other words, in this particular area shamanism reached a plane of development and refinement unknown elsewhere. One might call those who had brought it about 'the supershamans'.

Such a body would rapidly gain a reputation for wisdom extending far beyond its own boundaries. Naturally, their nearest neighbours would have been those most readily and most deeply influenced and would have received that influence in its purest form. It may also have happened that, under the impetus of some natural cataclysm, at least a portion of the peoples among whom the 'supershamans' practised were forced to migrate, carrying their knowledge to new areas. In any event, rumour of their extraordinary capabilities would have been conveyed through trade and travellers' tales, so that even those furthest away would have picked up crumbs from the storehouse, absorbing them into their own shamanic systems and thereby accounting for widely diffused similarities.

The selfsame rumours could also have reached even those who regarded themselves as both educated and civilized, inspiring a deep curiosity, a burning desire to discover the *terra mirabilis* and its inhabitants.

The obvious objection is that in those places where shamanism still survives there is no hint of any kind of institutional body, so what possible licence do we have for such a theory?

In *The Lives and Opinions of the Eminent Philosophers,* Diogenes Laertius quotes from two lost works, the *Mageia* of Aristotle and *The Succession of the Philosophers* by Sotion of Alexandria. What he borrows therefrom is a list of the founders of philosophy which includes the Persian Magi, the priesthoods of the Babylonians, an Indian body he calls the 'Gymnosophists' (meaning Naked Wise Men, obviously Yogi) and the Druids.

All four had a shamanistic ancestry; all four were, to a greater or less degree, organized bodies. The Mesopotamian priesthoods show a uniformity in belief, practice and knowledge. So do the Persian Magi. As to the Druids our knowledge is exiguous, but even if we ignore Caesar's controversial account of an annual convention in the country of the Carnutes (an area centering on the Loire Valley), there are signs of an organization which transcended the normal tribal frontiers. We know they could cross them even in times of war and, according to Strabo, they were able to intervene to stop battles. Dedications to similar gods found all over the Celtic cultural province testify to a homogeneity of belief. We also know of Druidic colleges or *bangors* commemorated in two British placenames, further evidence that Druidism, though shamanistic, was also a unified belief-system.

What of the Indian Yogi? Certainly, they exhibit an almost idiosyncratic degree of individualism, yet beneath it is also a consistency in beliefs. What is more there is, as between the Persians, Celts and Indians, a remarkable similarity in them.

Since they are racially related, they could have held them before their dispersal. On the other hand, this fails to account for the Semitic Babylonians who shared it at least in part. If they all received them from the same source, they must have done so separately.

What and where was it?

Perhaps there is an intimation in the Greek myths of a golden age and of the Hyperboreans as the last survivors of it. The Hyperboreans sound very much like 'Supershamans' and it was to their land that Apollo returned each winter, one reason why Greek travellers such as the seventh-century Aristeas set off in quest of it.

For our information about Aristeas, we are dependent mainly on Herodotus. He tells us that he was associated with the attribute of the Hyperborean Apollo, the raven, and that he came from Proconnesus, an island in the Sea of Marmara. Among the Greek colonies on both sides of the Sea of Marmara the cult of Hyperborean Apollo was particularly well entrenched. Abaris, the mysterious figure said to have been sent to Pythagoras on Apollo's instruction, is described by Herodotus as 'a Hyperborean'. This leads some writers to call him a Druid, an assumption which may have arisen from the fact that the Land of the Hyperboreans was equated with Britain in one highly ambiguous reference. More probably he was a priest from one of the temples of Apollo in the Marmara region.

Aristeas's journey took him as far as Scythic territory where he was told more about the Hyperboreans. His hosts could be expected to be well informed for, besides those Scythic tribes he met, the successors of those who had migrated south-westward to colonize an area to the north of the Black Sea, there was another hundreds of miles to the north-east and the two communities were in touch with one another.

They told him that the Hyperboreans lived beyond a range of gold-bearing mountains guarded by griffons. The gold-bearing mountains must have been those of the Altaic Range, for Altai means 'golden' and the metal is still worked there. We, may therefore conclude that the Land of the Hyperboreans, if it ever existed, lay beyond the Altaic Range.

As the area is one several thousand square miles in extent and

accommodated many different peoples – among them the
Scythes just mentioned – it is hardly a precise location. And we
have still failed to connect them with the four bodies mentioned
by Diogenes, the Persian Magi, the Babylonic priesthood, the
Indian Yogi or the Druids.

Perhaps we can turn for guidance to that other Greek
traveller, Pythagoras, whose journeys, made with the objective of
acquiring occult or esoteric knowledge, took him in the direction
of Egypt, Persia and Mesopotamia. Why did he choose to go
eastward rather than northward for, like Aristeas, he, too,
accorded special veneration to the Hyperborean Apollo and
could be expected to want to know more about him.

Among the few opinions about this mysterious god on which
scholars are unanimous is that, although his name seems to be
Greek (there is dispute over its meaning), he was not one of the
original Olympians.

One view is that he is a rechristened version of the
Mesopotamian Shamash, originally Sumerian. Undoubtedly
Shamash resembled Apollo in several ways. He was solar; he
had once been a shepherd; he was the ruler of oracles. There
are, however, almost as many dissimilarities as resemblances.
Shamash was a god of justice. His attribute was a bull, a creature
nowhere associated with Apollo, and, in the very activity where,
if borrowing had taken place, one would expect imitation to be
exact, the craft of divination, there is nothing of the kind. The
Mesopotamian priesthoods, like the Etruscans, prophesied by
examining the entrails of animals; the prophecies of Apollo were
conveyed through human mediums. Furthermore, Shamash was
happily married and the father of divine offspring. All Apollo's
amours ended unhappily for him.

In place of a wife he had a twin sister, Artemis, who may, in
fact, be a useful, if circumstantial clue. Artemis is linked with
the bear, among other ways, through her name which contains
the ursine element *Arcte* ('Arctic' means 'the land of the bear')
and bears are usually born as twins, frequently a male and a
female. This, taken in conjunction with another known detail of
Apollo's lifestyle – his four-month absence from Delphi, a
period which matches that of hibernation – leads one to wonder
whether he may not have been a bear totem who had
metamorphosed into an anthropomorphic deity?

If he was, then to follow his track we must leave the Fertile
Crescent and, like Aristeas, go northward once more.

While travelling in that direction, if we should cast our eyes heavenward, sooner or later, the stars themselves would provide us with another reminder of the bear: the constellation we call – and so did the Greeks – the Great Bear, Ursa Major, pointing like a fingerpost to the Pole Star. And if Apollo's Delphic sanctuary was a Great Centre, the area below the Pole Star is surely an even greater one for it is, truly, the axis on which the disc of the earth rotates. Can it be, then, that Delphi became a second centre entirely by virtue of the presence there of the god who came from the primary centre?

Not far from Ursa Major is another constellation with a bear name, Ursa Minor and, although Artemis is primarily a moon deity the counterpart of her solar brother, she is also repeatedly linked with it.

Sometimes in books and articles on popular astronomy it is suggested that the derivation of the names of both constellations was due to the resemblance they were supposed to have to a bear. The true reason is that it was named in honour of the presiding deity of the region, a bear god, whose cult spread radially out from it. The Lapps of Northern Europe, who probably inhabited the area before travelling westwards, worshipped the bear and, if one goes eastward, he is to be found among the Ainu, the aboriginal inhabitants of the islands which are now Japan. The Celts had a bear god, too. They called him 'Mattu'. He occurs even in late myths as a Welsh king called 'Math', whom some believe to be the prototype of 'Arthur'.

For Geoffrey Ashe the seven stars of the Great Bear are the original of all the recurrent mystic heptads and if, as I believe, he is correct, then the region is obviously of very great significance.

And it is, of course, one where shamanism still abounds, indeed the very word 'shaman' comes from those who live in it. They call the shamanic trance 'flight on the Golden Arrow', the missile which the Divine Archer looses from his bow. Furthermore, as sun god, Apollo was also god of gold.

As it happens, the Hyperboreans were not exclusive to the Greeks. Cryptic references to mysterious northerners occur in Norse legend, while among the Celts, they are the *Tuatha de Danann,* the people of the goddess Danu, bringers of all manner of civilizing gifts. But it is among the Hindus that we find the closest parallels as well as the most frequent references to a northerly people they call the 'Kurus'.

There is another confirmation that we are on the right track. The Greeks associate the Hyperboreans with the Golden Age, the first and finest of the four through which the world has lived.

And Hindu mythology, too, has its four ages, the first and finest of which was the Age of Truth.

Buddhists and Hindus seem in no doubt about the location of the Kurus. It is on Mount Meru or Sumeru whose modern name is Mount Kailas, the highest peak in the Tibetan range which takes its name.

Mythologically it is the dwelling place of Seven Sages who have their reflection in the heavens: they are stars of the Great Bear. And, just as the Hyperboreans occur in other contexts, so too do the Seven Sages: the Persians and the Greeks had them. In the case of the last they were associated particularly with Apollo.

And to reach this area from the lands of the western Scythes, Aristeas would certainly have had to cross the Altaic Mountains.

But we have not yet exhausted the parallels between the Greek Apolline cults and Hinduism, for there is also the doctrine of reincarnation shared by Indians and Celts and adopted by the Orphics and Pythagoreans.

The Influence of Bon

When Buddhist missionaries arrived in Tibet from India in about the eighth century of our own era, they encountered the Bon magicians. They so impressed the visitors that they besought and were granted initiation into their mysteries. As a result Bon magic was absorbed into Tibetan Buddhism, with some of the lamas, or monks, maintaining and practising the old Bon wisdom. It includes prophecy, healing and the induction of trances in which the magician can separate soul from body to travel freely, not only in the physical, but also in the spirit, world.

The Indian Buddhists were not the first people to be influenced by Bon. About three hundred years earlier it had penetrated Hinduism, giving rise to Tantrism, while Chinese Taoism, whose beginnings go back much further, to the eighth century BC, was very largely Bon given the gloss of a philosophical system.

But it was – and still is, for there are remote areas of Tibet where Bon survives – more than a disparate collection of magical operations haphazardly passed on. There is a long-standing tradition of an academy of esoteric studies whose curriculum included such subjects as astronomy and mathematics, two of Pythagoras's greatest preoccupations and two of the activities for which both the Persian Magi and the Babylonians were famous not only in their own time, but through all history.

Campbell sees the Sumerians, predecessors of Babylonians

and Persians, as primarily responsible for these two developments. He believes them to have occurred in the Sumerian city-states about 3,500 BC concurrently with that period to which archaeology has assigned an abrupt increase in the size of the temple complexes of south Mesopotamia. The reason is, he says, the advent of the 'science of a new order of humanity . . . the professional, full-time, initiated, strictly regimented temple priest'. Developments of the kind we are discussing are, in other words, the product of an organized intelligentsia.

The problem is: had Sumerian knowledge evolved painfully *after* they had established themselves between the Tigris and Euphrates or had they brought it with them?

There is certainly evidence to suggest that Sumerian religion did not develop *in situ* in the city-states. The *Epic of Gilgamesh* shows markedly shamanistic influences and there is also their custom of building ziggurats. Not only did these represent the pivot of the universe – the Great Centre, recalling the Hindu and Buddhist Mount Meru, they also had seven tiers or storeys symbolizing the Seven Heavens.

The racial origins of the Sumerians are unknown, but on the basis of linguistic information, at best, it must be stressed, tenuous and debatable, they may have been a Mongoloid race. In other words, they too had had contact with the Altaic Zone and, in view of their advanced knowledge, perhaps with its secret academy. The twelve months of the Mesopotamian year are what we call the zodiac – even the word itself is of their coining. However it is surprising, if no more, to find that the Tibetans, too, have a zodiac which, like the Mesopotamian, divides the year into twelve 'houses'.

Conclusion

If there is any substance for the notion of 'Supershamans', in whose hands rudimentary ideas were converted into something quite different, it certainly seems to me that it is in the direction of the Altaic Zone that we should look for their traces.

In the previous chapter Theosophy and its belief in the Ancient Wisdom received passing mention. According to Helena Blavatsky, founder of the Theosophical Society, the Incarnate Masters who are its custodians came from Tibet.

11. Shamanism and the Major Religions

Even if one possessed suitable qualifications, to attempt to explain the influence of shamanism on the major religions in the space of a single chapter would be rather like trying to write the plot of *War and Peace* on the back of a postcard.* Excluding all but the main sects which have grown up within them, as, for example, Catholicism, Orthodoxy and Protestantism within Christianity, Shi'ism and Sufism in Islam, or the Orthodox, Reformed and Liberal synagogues in Judaism, the number remains daunting all have been marked by shamanism to greater or lesser degree and in different ways. Indeed, we have always seen how some characteristic motifs, such as a Narrow Bridge, are to be found in Christianity and Islam.

If one adds to the principal religions and their main sects those combinations found particularly in the Far East, such as Tantric-Buddhism or Shinto-Confucianism then the subject is one to which justice could hardly be done even in a doctoral thesis. The only excuse for attempting the task at all is to demonstrate, though in a random and perhaps capricious fashion, how deeply shamanism has permeated every aspect of human life.

There is, of course, a certain piquancy in its presence in any of the great religions, for one can picture a Buddhist or Muslim missionary evincing the same pitying contempt for those shamans they no doubt came across on their evangelizing travels as Victorian Christian missionaries undoubtedly did. Not, of course, that the shaman has been the only interloper in religion, for another has also been the communal and ecstatic practices of

---

* It is almost needless to point out that suggesting a religion contains shamanistic elements is no derogation of it, nor any reflection on the truth of its doctrines.

the fertility cults – a topic the late Monsignor Ronald Knox has treated exhaustively in *Enthusiasm*. Its influence on Christianity is plainly visible in movements such as Pentecostalism and the 'charismatic' sects.

In other cases, one finds a combination of influences at work. Total-immersion Baptists and other 'born again' Christian sects suggest shamanism, but often their religious worship is more reminiscent of the feminine cults. The same mixture can be detected in the rattlesnake-handling religions, such as those in remote areas of Tennessee. Rattlesnake-handling was practised by Indian medicine men who collected the creatures in the spring and, at special seances, placed them, in a sack, on the heads of tribal members. The sack obviously provided necessary protection from their fangs, but the shamans themselves used no such protection and took the reptiles in their bare hands, even allowing them to bite to show their magic immunity to the venom.

The obvious difference is that among the Christian snake-handling sects any worshipper can, if he or she wishes or feels 'moved' to do so, handle them, allowing them to climb over arms and body, and often faces. Before the climactic moment when the snakes are brought out the congregation participate in what is very much a 'revivalist' meeting with emotionally charged preaching and hymn-singing often attended by hand-clapping, dancing and involuntary shouts. While it is believed that the Holy Spirit protects the snake-handlers, in fact, they are frequently bitten, sometimes fatally, all such mishaps being blamed on failure of merit, if they manage to survive the experience, even by the sufferers themselves.

A similar combination of influences is at work in those Christian cults which use hallucinogens. The practice itself is shamanistic, but set in the environment of revivalist fun-damentalism.

One of these, founded by the North American Indian teacher, Jonathon Koshiway, as 'The Church of the First Born', encourages its members to use peyote in what is a kind of communion. However, drug-using cults are not restricted to the Indians, and have spread to black groups, the altered state of consciousness induced by the drug being regarded as the Holy Spirit manifesting himself within the individual.

The Major Religions: Two Groups

As a very broad generalization, and ignoring cross-currents and the effect of influences from common but, no doubt, extremely archaic sources, some of which have been discussed in preceding chapters, the major religions can be divided into two groups: a Middle Eastern group which comprises those such as Judaism, Christianity and Islam, and a Far Eastern one, much larger in number, which besides some obvious examples such as Hinduism and Buddhism, also numbers those such as Bon and Taoism.

Judaism and Christianity

In any examination of the traits of shamanism in religion it is perhaps only natural to begin with Judaism and Christianity as those are most familiar to the majority of westerners.

In the latter one can at once see the shamanistic elements in the life of its founder himself. He is a healer, but, according to the Gospel account appears to come into the full use of his powers only after his stay in the wilderness where he experienced a series of 'temptations'. Similar wilderness visits such as those of St Anthony with their accompanying 'temptations' also suggest shamanistic mediation.

Many commentators have also pointed out the death-and-rebirth elements in the Crucifixion and Resurrection.

In Judaism and Christianity one can, of course, see the male dominance which we have noted as characteristic of the shaman. The ruthless suppression of any manifestation which smacked of witchcraft has, throughout its history, been one of the functions of the Christian Church, and similar prohibitions on witchcraft are to be found in Judaism including the famous Biblical injunction, 'Do not suffer a witch to live', later used as licence for the slaughter of women by men.

The Jewish rite of circumcision and, particularly, that of Christian baptism have frequently been regarded as relics of the shamanistic rebirth.

Such desultory examples as we have so far adduced might appear to be no more than chance importations probably derived from those, such as the Mesopotamians, who helped to form Jewish religious ideas and hence those of Christianity, and one could accept such an interpretation were it not for evidence of a much deeper shamanistic penetration.

The books of Exodus and Leviticus contain an account of the series of face-to-face meetings between Yahweh and Moses (Fourteenth to Thirteenth century BC) on Mount Sinai which yielded not only the enormously influential Ten Commandments, but also the Laws of Kosher or ritual purity, still observed by pious Jews.

This kind of encounter between mortal and divine, involving a difficult ascent by the former, is plainly shamanistic, but there is more. A profoundly mystical and esoteric element in Judaism is represented by Kabbalism which developed out of an earlier Jewish tradition known as *Merkava*. Their beliefs include reincarnation and it is significant that, in Merkava particularly, stress was laid on the seven 'heavenly dwellings' which the soul had to pass through in its cycle of rebirths in order to ascend to the highest of all.

Although said to have been founded by none other than Moses himself, a magus of no mean ability as his successful duel with the Pharaonic magicians demonstrates, there is, in fact, no evidence for its existence before the first century AD and, in view of the late date, its real source was probably Greek Platonism. One of its most important Platonic centres after the conquests of Alexander in the fourth century BC was the Egyptian city of Alexandria whose cosmopolitan population included many Jews.

All the same, behind Merkava and Kabbalah lies the belief, probably much older, in a secret revelation from God to Moses which, in its turn was communicated orally to initiates selected because of their superior moral qualities and thereby transmitted to our own times. Those fortunate enough to be chosen place themselves in the hands of a master and, provided they follow his instructions meticulously and maintain a life of virtue, the Kabbala will give them direct access to the divine.

Among the means to attaining this end is gematria, an exclusively Hebraic form of numerology. Gematria is possible because the letters of the Hebrew alphabet double as numbers (an idea, like the Hebrew alphabet itself, borrowed from the Phoenicians). Thus, any word in Hebrew can be read simultaneously as a sequence of numbers. These, when added together, produce a total used in further gematric operations.

Its main application has been in scriptural exegesis with Kabbalists believing that through it many of the Bible's more obscure passages become comprehensible. Hence, gematrically, the word 'Sinai' is equal to the Hebrew word for 'ladder'. That is to say, if the letters making up each word are read as numbers their sum is the same in both cases. This would be no more than a coincidence were it not that the two interchangeable images lie at the heart of Kabbalism. One is the tree; the other, the ladder, both common metaphors for the shaman's journey. Like the shamanic ladder, that of the Kabbalists links the three worlds, as demonstrated in Jacob's dream. In this way, the gematric correspondence between Sinai, repeatedly referred to in scripture as 'the Holy' or 'God's Mountain', and the ladder is no coincidence; it is the key to the passages in Exodus and Leviticus, and tells us that Moses's visits to the mountain are, indeed, shamanic ascents.

The fact that Mount Zion, like Mount Sinai, was a world centre has already ben noted, but there is another shamanistic relic in the Hebrew word *bethel*, literally 'house of the Lord'. Besides being the name of the ancient city situated north of Jerusalem, it can also stand for a hallowed spot and for the pillar or stone marking it, thus giving it an affinity with the omphalos stone at Delphi and all the other stones which mark centres.

It is a bethel that Jacob rests his head on in the sleep in which his ladder-vision came to him, implying that intrinsic magic within the stone induces it. The theme of a sacred site causing a sleeper to see a vision is, of course, a common one occurring, among other places, in the context of Christian mysticism.

Islam

In Islam, the other main religion in the Middle Eastern group, shamanistic antecedents are still plainer and may have been introduced by the pre-Islamic Bedouin with whom Mohammed was fostered in childhood and had later to turn to for refuge while fleeing the hostility of the Meccans.

They may also be the source of the many other shamanistic elements in the life of the Prophet. Thus, we are told that while meditating on a mountain near Mecca, he received a revelation from God through the archangel Gabriel. In some versions Gabriel is said to have slit him from neck to waist and removed and washed his heart before returning it to his body.

In another legend Mohammed makes a night journey to Paradise. In some versions he is said to have been conveyed thither on a creature with a woman's face, a mule's body and peacock's tail. In others, he climbs a ladder which rises up from the temple in Jerusalem. In both, he passes through Seven Heavens on his way to his destination and, during his visit, meets many of the biblical patriarchs, including Moses, Jesus and Abraham.

Mohammed is also, like Moses, a master of water, conjuring up a well to assist one of the desert tribes who befriend him, while examples of his miracle-working include his making the dry ewe give milk.

The same shamanistic footprint is on other aspects of Islam. The Ka'abah-stone at Mecca, actually a shrine before the rise of Islam but now enclosed by the Great Mosque, is the object of the pilgrimage all Muslims hope to make. It is plainly a centre and it is significant that the faithful are required to circumambulate it seven times. The seven-motif recurs in the ascent of the devout soul to God which involves mounting seven successive steps – representing penitence, abstinence, renunciation, poverty, patience, faith and satisfaction.

But seven-mystique is carried to its apogee among the Ismailis, a branch of Shi'ah, which enjoyed its greatest popularity from the Ninth to Thirteenth centuries of our own era. The Ismailis regard the Koran in the same way as the Kabbalists do the Talmud, that is to say as open to two interpretations, an exoteric and esoteric one. The latter was available only to initiates through a hierarchic organization led by an *imam*, a successor of a founding *imam* whose reincarnation the devout await.

In Ismaili theology the universe is believed to be a cyclic process ruled by the number seven with seven 'speakers' or bringers of divine revelation appearing before each new epoch. The last speaker is Mohammed himself who was followed by seven *imams*. Although during this century its spiritual head, the Aga Khan, has taken measures to bring the Ismailis nearer to mainstream Islam, unlike other Muslims they still do not worship in mosques but in so-called 'houses of gathering' and their actual modes of worship bear little resemblance to those in wider usage.

Another group, also a branch of Shi'ah, are the numerically small Druse who, like the Ismaili Muslims, have an esoteric doctrine and, like the Kabbalists, believe in reincarnation.

Sufism, a specifically Islamic form of mysticism, is sometimes regarded as shamanistic, but is actually more closely allied to religious mysticism. This, in contrast, to esoteric systems, believes that communion with the divine is attainable only through pious meditation and selfless love of it.

Buddhism and Hinduism

That the marks of shamanism lie deepest on the Far Eastern religions is indisputable. It thus gives them the appearance of having received them at first – where others received them at second-hand and, although there were undoubtedly others, one of the most important of these original sources was probably Tibetan Bon.

In the previous chapter we discussed the possibility of an area centering on Mount Kailas, the home of the Hindus' Seven Sages, as the homeland of what I dubbed the 'supershamans'. It would, none the less, be hazardous to assert that it was precisely coterminous with Tibet as it is now known and even more so to assume Bon was the original basis of the teachings of the supershamans, if they ever existed. Bon may itself have been derived from or influenced by others' belief-systems. Despite the fact that it survives in some parts of Bhutan, Sikkim and on the northern and eastern borders of Tibet itself there can be little doubt, if the evidence is to be believed, that it is in a considerably degraded form. Something nearer to original Bon is probably to be found in the magical practices of Tibetan Buddhism as these have been described by writers like Alexandra David-Neel.

Buddhism, in any case, has its own shamanistic character. Gautama Buddha himself underwent the typical experience of solitary contemplation in the wilderness in his search for enlightenment. According to legend, after defeating Mara, the evil one, by his superior reasoning Buddha spent the night meditating under a banyan tree. In the first watch he acquired insight into his former incarnations. In the middle watch, he attained the 'divine eye', enabling him to see the passing away and rebirth of all things, and in the last attained full enlightenment with the realization of the Four Noble Truths: the Truth of misery; the Truth that misery originates in desire; that it can be eliminated by eliminating desire; and, fourthly, that it can be eliminated by following the methodical way.

Buddhism itself evolved against a Hindu background. A hundred and eight Brahmins visited the infant Gautama five days after his birth and predicted that he would become either a monarch or a Buddha. After his achievement of Enlightenment he was begged by the Hindu deity Indra and by Brahma himself to preach to the world.

The references in Hindu mythology to the Land of the Kurus and the identification of the home of the Seven Sages with Mount Kailas suggest that Hinduism may itself have been influenced by Bon. However, this can only have been one of several forces which helped to shape it. The Indo-European invaders of the Indian sub-continent brought with them their own beliefs, though these may have been touched by Bon while they were still in their original homelands. Wherever they went, the migrants must have come into contact with the religions of the autochthonous populations. As the Greek tribes encountered that of the Pelasgians, so the 'Aryan' invaders of India encountered that of the remnants of the Indus Valley civilization, though it was already past its heyday when they arrived. However, these religions were themselves to a greater or lesser degree shamanistic, so that for those examining the evidence at this distance of time it becomes difficult to assign which influence came from where with any confidence.

The presence of the shaman in Hinduism is, however, incontestable, as no one reading the *Vedas* can fail to recognize. We are told, for example, that the *Muni* (the word actually means 'ecstatic') were able to 'mount the wind', a choice of words which turns the wind into a shamanic horse.

In the opinion of some scholars, the *Muni* were the predecessors of the Yogi, whom we have identified with the Greeks' 'Gymnosophists' or Naked Wise Men. Though undoubtedly affected by the beliefs of other cultures and, especially those of Hinduism, Yoga may have roots in Indo-European ideas. The use of breath-control as an aid to trance-induction is found in several contexts. The similarity between the Greek *phrenes*, lungs, and the Sanskrit *prana*, breath, was noted earlier and the traditional yogic 'lotus position', now exclusively associated with Eastern mysticism, was normal to most Indo-European peoples. Celtic epigraphy yields a number of examples, including the famous representation of the Horned God, Cernunnos, on the Gundestrupp Cauldron.

Shamanistic characteristics are equally common in Brahminism. In a typical rite, the sacrificer climbs to heaven on a symbolical ladder. Max Weber in *The Religion of India* describes the Brahmins as a caste of magicians who evolved into princely advisers on ritual and portents. The mythological evidence makes it plain that the Druids occupied much the same role in Celtic society and the late Professor Miles Dillon has shown that there are so many parallels between Brahminism and Druidism that it is almost certain that the two bodies developed from the same Indo-European nucleus.

Tantism and Taoism

There is no doubt, however, that the most shamanistic of the Indian religions is Tantrism which, of course, exists in both Hindu and Buddhist forms. Tantrism teaches the existence of seven *chakras* or seats of power within the body (analogous beliefs are to be found in Yoga), and that these are a microcosm of the universe itself.

The Tantric initiate places himself under the tutelage of a master who directs his endeavours and teaches him its secret, esoteric doctrine. The fact that the priests of Buddhist Tantrism include a small drum in the equipment of their calling is a further hint of their ancestry.

However, the sexual rituals of Tantrism in which copulation, *maithuna,* is regarded as the symbolic attainment of Enlightenment, has suggested to some the influence of Taoism which also extols the sexual act as spiritually beneficial for both women and men.

Taoism is, in fact, the shamanistic system least marked by an antipathy for the feminine. Its antimonies of Yin and Yang, broadly masculine and feminine, though opposites, are complementary.* Hence, in the standard symbol of the divided circle the Yin or dark area has its spot of Yang, and the light, Yang area its spot of Yin. While woman may be Yin, she needs constantly to recharge her Yang and the reverse applies to the man. Any contact with the opposite force will do this to some extent, but the greatest transfer takes place in the sexual act itself.

Tao literally means 'the way' and the way is that of the natural forces. The Taoist's aim was to make himself one with nature, to let its pulses course through his body and mind. To this end yogic exercises, gymnastics, magic elixirs prepared by alchemists, dietary rules and a variety of sexual activities were used with the aim of improving vitality and, ultimately, of creating an immortal body so refined it could leave the mortal body to partake in the bliss of paradise. A being who reached such an exalted state was *hsien,* a word that connotes taking flight from the material world and escaping spatial restrictions. The immortal *hsien* were called the 'feathered people', and their winged or feathered images appear in the art of the period.

The traditional founder of Taoism was the sixth century BC Chinese sage Lao Tzu, author of the *Tao Te Ching.* This consists of a series of poems so obscure and aphoristic that one could interpret them in almost any way one chose and the second great Taoist classic, the *Chuang Tzu,* attributed to the fourth century Chuang Chou, was probably more responsible

---

* The antimonies of Pythagoreanism, with which they are sometimes compared, may conceivably have the same root, but are antithetical to one another.

for developing it into a unified system.

However, shamanism is so deeply imbedded in the history of China that attributing its beginnings to a single founder or to a particular philosophy can only be arbitrary. A picture of the legendary sovereign Fu Hsi of the Third Millennium BC shows a figure dressed in leopard and bear skins, seated on a rock, contemplating a tortoise which gazes reverentially up at him. Laid out on the ground are the eight hexagrams of the *I Ching* said to have been inspired by the patterns on tortoiseshell.

Whether Taoism had direct contact with Bon or whether both had a common ancestor is a much debated topic. However, the plainly shamanistic bases of all the Eastern religions, the often close resemblances between them and their tendency to form combinations has, over the centuries, led to a blurring of many of the differences, for instance, of those of Hinduism and Buddhism. Furthermore, in contrast with the often violent competitive hostility found among the religions of the Middle Eastern group, the Far Eastern ones have tended to be mutually tolerant. Their attitudes to one another are well summed up in an article on Korean religion in *The Korea Newsletter* for September 1984:

> When Buddhism and Confucianism entered Korea from Asia neither considered itself to be in conflict with the other nor in opposition to rites relating to local nature spirits.

Admirable and indeed enviable as this tolerance may appear to those accustomed to deep mutual antagonism between religions, it makes it difficult to trace particular ideas or practices to their origins with any certainty.

Gnosticism

If the traces of shamanism in the major religions would provide substance for a thesis, their occurrence in the great heresies could occupy a whole library and no treatment of them here can be more than superficial, almost to the point of frivolity.

Behind many of the major heresies lies Gnosticism which began to appear in the scond century AD and consisted of a mixture of influences including that of dualism derived from Persian Zoroastrianism. Dualists believed in two creations, a spiritual one emanating from God and a physical one emanating from Satan, so that the first was inherently good, the second inherently evil. The two were locked in a ceaseless struggle which obviously brings to mind that between the Titanic and the Divine in Orphism.

But what marks Gnosticism as undoubtedly shamanistic is its belief in a body of esoteric knowledge available only to an elite, and, in particular, its encouragement of the use of trance as a means of gaining insight into the sacred.

Many of the Gnostic teachings, and especially its dualism, were absorbed into Manichaeism. Long regarded as a Christian heresy, it was more properly a religion in its own right though one which shared Christian beliefs. From about the fourth century, isolated, minor Christian sects which adopted Gnostic or Manichaean dualism were constantly appearing and withering away, often without any intervention from orthodoxy. Among the more important were the Bogomils and the Paulicians, who flourished from the tenth to the fifteenth centuries.

All these movements were the predecessors of the Albigensians or Cathars (meaning The Pure) which gained a large popular following mainly in the Languedoc from about the end of the eleventh century. The dualistic character of Catharism was the one for which it is best known and was the cause of the persecution of the sect by the Catholic Church, for the belief that the physical and fleshly were evil entailed the denial of such basic doctrines as the Incarnation.

However, there was another aspect of Catharism to which the French scholar, Rene Nelli has drawn attention. This is its body of secret doctrine, available only to the 'Perfects', those set apart from ordinary 'Believers' through their having undergone an initiatory ritual.

Though the ecclesiastical proscriptions on their teachings combined with their own extreme secrecy mean that almost nothing of them has survived, there is one intriguing snippet of information.

The castle of Montsegur, on the summit of a hill in the Arriege, which served as spiritual bastion of the movement for most of its existence, incorporated into its design elements, such as a pentagonal plan, which are associated with magic rather than Christianity. The fall of the castle in 1247 spelt the end of Catharism by delivering its leaders into the hands of the Inquisition. Yet, according to a local legend, not all died at the stake. Some managed to escape to find sanctuary in – of all places – Tibet.

On the face of it what we have here is simply one of those

'survival' myths which tend to grow up in such situations and of which Napoleon I and the Tsar Nicholas and the Russian Royal Family have, in their time, been the subject. On the other hand, the legend of a link between Montsegur and Tibet has a very long history* and some credibility has been given to it by the discovery in the 'thirties of a document written in a script at first taken for Arabic, then Chinese, but finally believed to be Tibetan.

---

* There are also stories of visitors to it who have encountered apparitions of oriental-looking figures wearing the saffron robe.

12. Shamanism and the Modern World

How should we assess shamanism? Is it, as its supporters would claim, something of great antiquity which has in it much that could serve us? Or is it, as others would say, no more than crude, superstitious delusion? Is the shaman himself mentally sick?

There is no doubt that, as we saw in Chapter 3, in some societies hysteria or epilepsy* is regarded as a sign from the spirits that the sufferer has been chosen to be a shaman. At the same time, critics have pointed out that the trance comes into the category of an altered state of consciousness, and like others, can be induced through drugs or by hypnotic suggestion, neither of which has much to do with intervention by the spirits.

However, the fact that in some societies it is the prerogative of those who are mentally ill by no means discredits shamanism as a whole. It could mean, for instance, that in these particular places it has fallen into decay and there is evidence that this is the case.

As to the shaman himself, of those who have encountered him in his native habitat, some believe him to show mental abnormality, while a second, equally large group, holds the opposite view, and a more rational third comes down in favour of the mean: that, though some shamans are no doubt suffering from mental instability of one form or another, others radiate an aura of vigorous, cheerful and extrovert normality.

In any event, categorizing shamanism as mental illness plainly

---

* If the shaman is an epileptic then he is in good company, for as a group, they have included some of history's most outstanding men and women. Joan of Arc has been so categorized on account of her 'voices', while others include Julius Caesar, probably St Paul and possibly Shakespeare.

raises questions of definition and here we find little consensus even among practising psychologists. Illness is a divergence from the healthy or normal state of the organism, a condition easily enough recognized in the case of the physical where pain, fever, an altered pulse-rate or other symptoms are present. But what is 'normal' and 'healthy' in the sphere of mind or spirit? Is the society in which we live itself so normal or healthy as to provide the criteria by which we can assess departures from it?

And the symptoms of mental illness are by no means as straightforward or as unambiguous as those of physical ones. For example, it is characteristic of some conditions that the sufferer displays a highly developed insight into the motivation of others. Ironically enough, this is the very quality the psychiatrist himself seeks to cultivate and the more he is able to, the more successful he is likely to be in his calling. In other words, what is abnormal in the patient is, not merely normal but actually desirable in his therapist, a point well made in Peter Shaffer's play *Equus* where the youth, Alan Strang, undergoing treatment at the hands of the psychiatrist, Martin Dysart, early on his therapy successfully taunts him with the fact he has ceased to have sexual relations with his wife.

An analogous situation arises with shamanism. Some mental patients appear to possess what can only be regarded as clairvoyance, sometimes to startling degree. The shaman also claims or is credited with clairvoyant gifts, but if we are to regard him as mentally sick on account of this, are we to regard the psychiatrist as mentally sick because he possesses the same insight into motivation as his patient?

Of course, attempts to discredit mystical manifestations are far from new and there are, to be sure, those who have a vested interest in doing so by whatever means may lie to hand, for if the shaman's beliefs have even a grain of validity, then they threaten the fabric of the rationalist and materialist determinism which is the true mythology of our times. Revealed as an undiagnosed neuropath his threat is neutralized and he becomes something very much like 'the benighted primitive' whose 'conversion' was the target of nineteenth-century missionary zeal.

Nevertheless, it would be facile to dismiss the various explanations advanced to account for shamanism without scrutiny.

Among them is that it is a condition induced by the so-called 'Arctic sickness', a state of dissociation resulting from long exposure to sub-zero temperatures and icy, snow-swept landscapes. We know that it occurs among those who inhabit such wastes, the Eskimo or the nomad of the Siberian steppe. However, it is by no means restricted to them for it has afflicted European explorers. One of its symptoms is the sense of an illusory companion who may accompany the traveller for many miles before he disappears or is replaced by another escort. This certainly has its shamanistic overtones, but it is hard to see how Arctic sickness could account for Australian, Central American or African shamanism, let alone its incidence among the sunlit landscapes of the Mediterranean.

Shamanism and Schizophrenia

The fashionable contemporary explanation is that the shaman is a schizophrenic, and, to be sure, there are many similarities. Not only do both exhibit a sometimes startling insight but, like the shaman, the schizophrenic is convinced of the reality of external, invisible presences.

However, on closer inspection the similarities become more superficial than real. The schizophrenic's apparent insights arise from an almost random grasping for sense in a chaotic and disorienting world where he seems to have lost the abilty to make sense even of that familiar but narrow band of reality which represents the picture of the universe most of us know. His is a world-view characterized by fragmentation and lack of structural unity.

By contrast, the shaman perceives his environment as a whole – indeed, if we are to believe our witnesses, as more *completely* whole than most of us; for him 'things fit together better'. Far from fitting together, the environment of the schizophrenic seems to be flying apart.

Furthermore, the structures of shamanism are consistent and, in very many ways, unvarying between one culture and another. Those of the schizophrenic are individual and idiosyncratic.

But what of the shamanic ecstasy which, in many ways, seems to resemble the crises of schizophrenia?

Again at close range they show more differences than affinities. For the crises of the mentally disturbed are unrelieved pain; repetition is to be avoided at all costs – the precise reason why he goes to a psychiatrist for help. By contrast, the shaman actually cultivates his crisis.

Of course, it can be argued that these differences of attitude arise from cultural conditioning. Our own culture tends to see altered states of consciousness, especially those occurring spontaneously, that is to say, without the stimulus of drugs or some other exogenous factor, as to some extent aberrant, often, in themselves, as symptomatic of mental illness. Those in whom they occur are therefore haunted by a fear of incipient madness. In other societies they are taken as signifying that the subject stands in a special relationship with the universal forces and so are socially advantageous.

But the actual content of the schizophrenic's experience must lead to the conclusion that it is qualitatively different from the shaman's. As a psychiatrist friend put it, 'No one who has seen a schizophrenic *in extremis* can doubt that, whatever social conditioning may cause, his experience is itself horrifying and agonising beyond words.'

The forces by which the schizophrenic is surrounded are never anything but threatening and – particularly – destructive. For the shaman, though threats exist, those forces with whom he deals are positive and *con*structive. Even in the 'summoning' phase, when the prospective shaman may seek to resist the bidding of the spirits with all his will-power, his relationship with them can at least be said to be ambivalent. The torment of the shamanic illness is counterbalanced by the promised reward when he obeys. No such hope is held out to the schizophrenic who, in consequence, wants nothing more than the removal of his persecutors.

Nor is the recognition of mental sickness the monopoly of our own society. Among some of the Sudanese tribes, for example, it is clearly distinguished from the shamanic experience. In other cases, because the resemblance of shamanism to morbid symptoms is recognized, the shaman is not allowed to practice until a year after his initial crisis.

Perhaps the most balanced view is that of Joseph Campbell who regards shamanism as a 'schizophrenia' with remissions, that is to say one which is under the shaman's control. And one might keep in mind Eliade's observation that if we find certain shamans displaying the indisputable symptoms of mental sickness it is only what we should expect since all shamans dwell in a twilight zone fraught with mental and spiritual perils, making it certain that some would succumb to them.

We might also take our minds back to Plato's Simile of the Cave and complete what we began in Chapter 1. As we saw then, the prisoner who fleetingly glimpsed the world outside the cave had his vision of reality transformed. But his short escape also affects his fellow-prisoners. When he tells them what he has seen all they can do is shake pitying heads. He can only have become deranged by his experience, for who but a madman would believe that such things as he describes could actually exist?

Extra Sensory Awareness

In Chapter 9 we considered the kind of situation in which the shamanistic can reappear as a popular movement and saw that it was usually at those moments when an accepted image of the universe and the human destiny contained in it are under the harshest criticism as in sixth-century ancient Greece, the Renaissance or our own era.

It is equally true that it tends to diminish in importance once these periods are over. Does this mean that it is itself as abnormal as the times which have spawned it? Or does it have positive, beneficial qualities, lessons for us we could fruitfully apply?

I believe that it does.

Thousands of years before Anton Mesmer introduced his 'Animal Magnetism' to late-eighteenth-century Paris, hypnotism was being used by shamans. It vanished when, like medicine, it was proscribed by the Church as belonging to magic and witchcraft. In Mesmer's own time, the scientific establishment dismissed his activities as charlatanism and delusion unworthy even of investigation. The introduction of hypnotism into medicine, surgery and psychiatry is wholly due to the efforts of men such as Charcot in Paris and James Braid in Manchester who were prepared to examine it dispassionately.

What applies to one sphere of the shaman's activities may well apply to others. One is the 'paranormal' with which he has always been associated. Another is radiesthesia which under its various less technical names of 'dowsing' and 'water divining' has also been with us for centuries, if not millennia. Both deserve, and to some extent are receiving, thorough, rigorous but unprejudiced scientific examination.

There is, however, an aspect more important than either of these. The shaman sees himself as in touch with forces not apprehensible to the generality of men. That he sees them in terms of 'power animals', spirits or gods, gigantic humans, is beside the point since, as we saw, men and women have always and continue to conceive the unknown in terms of the known.

It has to be said that in the present state of scientific and especially of physical knowledge, the notion that *in some form* such forces exist is more rather than less likely. The universe has been charged with electro-magnetic energy throughout its entire existence, yet to have suggested to a mid-Victorian that the very air we breathe is charged with energized particles, travelling at thousands of miles a second, capable of penetrating brick walls would have been to invite incarceration in an asylum. It was not until the development of radio and television that their existence came to be recognized.

Secondly, there is nothing inherently implausible about the idea of individuals who are more sensitive to the natural forces than others. It is known that sensitivity to electric current, for example, varies widely from person to person. A charge of such low power that most people can be quite unaware of it will be felt by others as a tingle through hands and arms uncomfortable enough to make them drop whatever is causing it, even if, as once happened to me, it was an expensive and well-insulated piece of broadcasting equipment.

The fact is that all our senses are 'tuned' and incapable of receiving the entire range of available 'signals'. For instance, if we were dependent wholly on our sense of sight, we should conclude that the spectrum consists simply of a band of seven colours with violet at the top and red at the bottom. As we know from other evidence, beyond these visible extremes lie ultra violet and infra red, giving them these somewhat bizarre names, which mean 'above violet' and 'below red', because we cannot see them. There are, besides, sounds below and above the range of the human auditory sense which are perfectly audible to a dog.

But our 'tuning' may actually be much finer than we realize. Sounds or smells, not normally audible, may in certain situations cause a physical reaction which suggests that at some level of the mind they are actually being received. Recent research suggests that one factor in sexual attraction may be smell. Those to whom we are drawn emit a subtle odour whose presence is registered by the senses, but below the threshold of consciousness.

The senses operating below the level of the consciousness may account for those occasions when we are suddenly alerted to an emergency, quite unaware of what has done so. We feel unaccountably impelled to turn round and only after doing so see the attacker creeping up behind us. A single-handed transatlantic yachtsman, sound asleep in his bunk after the exertions of the day, will startle into complete apprehensive wakefulness; a driver senses something wrong with his vehicle, without knowing why.

Under hypnosis it has often been possible to discover the cause. An infinitesimally small change in the character of the reflected light caused by his shadow betrays the approaching assailant; a normally inaudible alteration in the creak of the mast or of the car's engine note stimulates appropriate reactions by the organism in each case.

It has also been found that hypnotic suggestion can be used to increase this sensitivity dramatically. And it is, of course, recognized that those whose working lives bring them into a closer relationship with the natural environment, such as sailors, farmers and those living in less urbanized cultures than our own, have a far greater sensitivity to changes in it.

None the less, within the limits of the normal human sensory range there are those inviduals who are far more acute than others, who can hear the high-pitched squeak which the bat uses to guide itself in the dark. The picture of the universe formed by these hyperacuitives is obviously more detailed than that most of us form. In many ways, it must also be different in quality, even if the difference is no more than that of seeing a room as ill-lit or well-lit. In the latter case, an object we believed we had identified as one thing may well turn out to be quite another.

Hence, from one aspect the shaman may perhaps be seen as one who, naturally hyperacuitive, has trained his senses to a far greater degree than others. It may be this that lies behind his unusual rapport with his environment.

Shamanic Therapy

Of course, such a reductionist explanation as I have here offered is not one which would find much accord among those who have adopted shamanism and are actively trying to reintroduce it into our lives.

For many of them, the principal value of the shaman to his community is as a healer, both physical and mental.

Michael Harner sees shamanistic healing as an adjunct to orthodox methods. Dr Leslie Gray records that one of the factors which drew her towards shamanism was a car accident. Left severely injured, she was told by a succession of surgeons that nothing more could be done for her. In despair she went to an American Indian medicine man. His treatment was successful and, freed of pain herself, she besought instruction at his hands so that she could cure others.

To the sceptical Westerner the idea, axiomatic to the shaman that disease is due to malign intrusions or soul-loss is a difficult one to take seriously. However, since shamanic healing appears to work, at any rate for some individuals, one cannot help suspecting that it operates through the psyche. We now recognize that much illness is psychosomatic; it may be that shamanic therapy has a valuable part to play in reducing the sum of human suffering.

Indeed, to some extent it can be said that it is already doing so since altered states of consciousness induced by a multiplicity of means are playing an increasingly important role in the treatment of the mentally sick.

The wide use now made of dream therapy, particularly by Jungian psychologists who frequently interpret dream symbols in what might well be called 'magical terms', would also be the kind of treatment one might expect the shaman to employ even if his actual methodology differs from that to which we are accustomed.

In one way one cannot but agree with Leslie Gray who, when asked by an interviewer from the American *Yoga Journal* how shamanism was to be compared with traditional psychotherapy, answered, 'Oh, but shamanism is the traditional psychotherapy.'

Beyond the Conscious
There is another aspect of shamanism whose potential value to us as a tool we might consider.

The myths of the Divine Gifts – of Prometheus, Odin, Hephaistos or Quetzalcoatl – are to be found in every culture. Can it be that what they commemorate is the shaman acquiring knowledge via trance?

Extravagant as the notion might seem to be, perhaps we should recall what we know of the way in which many scientists from Newton and his apple to Albert Einstein, achieved their greatest insights. Jung quotes the examples of the French mathematician Henri Poincare who, during a sleepless night, saw mathematical symbols colliding until they formed a connection. There is also the case of the German chemist Friedrich Kekule who 'dreamt' of the molecular structure of benzine in the form of a snake with its tail in its mouth – incidentally an age-old shamanic symbol. He correctly interpreted this to mean that the benzine molecule was a closed carbon ring.

That in all these cases the subject was in a partially altered state of consciousness may or may not be a vindication of the shaman and his trance, but it suggests that in certain of these states the intuitive faculty becomes so much more acute that it is possible to make intuitive leaps of far greater magnitude than those possible in the normal state.

Perhaps we can justifiably go a little further and speculate whether they do not hint at the existence of a level of mind somewhat akin to the Jungian Collective Unconscious which can be reached by this route?

One need hardly add that it would correspond with beliefs the shaman has always held and which are still held in the East.

An Awareness of the Natural

Perhaps it has one other lesson. Industrial pollution, over-exploitation of the earth through bad farming methods or profligacy with chemical fertilizers, have become major preoccupations of our time. Part of the same syndrome, in the view of a growing number of people, is the use of drugs with unpredictable side-effects. The shaman might say that it has all come about because we have ceased to apprehend the overall unity of the universe and to direct our actions by it.

And his belief in a Cosmos has recently gained scientific backing. James Lovelock has propounded the theory that the earth is held in dynamic balance precisely because of the existence of life upon it. For example, it is the ability of plants and animals to convert one gas into another which maintains the equilibrium of the chemosphere and ionosphere, the earth's two protective layers, against the sun's all-devouring heat. As Dr Lovelock himself points out, the implication is that there are not two sciences, geology, concerned with the physical formation of the earth, and biology, concerned with life upon it, but one.

Again the shaman might nod agreement.

That such partnership with the Cosmos can help us avoid disaster is shown by one very telling example. In 1975, the people living in the Hai Cheng region of China were able to warn the authorities, some ten months before it occurred, that a serious earthquake was to be expected. The warning was heeded and a mass evacuation organized with the consequence that when the earthquake struck no casualties occurred, a point of which the Chinese government made much, claiming it was due to the superiority of Marxism.

However, Marxism was unable to save the inhabitants of the city of Tang Shan a year later. Half a million people were killed or injured.

The truth is that Hai Cheng was a remote rural area whose population were still deeply imbued with the shamanistic ideas of Taoism. They interpreted with perfect accuracy a host of natural signs – the uneasiness of the deer, the water level of the wells, the laying habits of the poultry – as presaging a natural cataclysm. Tang Shan, by contrast, was a large industrial city for whose inhabitants such things were rustic superstition.

Select Bibliography

Anisimov, A. E., *Cosmological Aspects of the Peoples of the North*, Toronto, 1963.
——, *Shaman's Tent of the Evenks*, Toronto, 1960.
Ashe, Geoffrey, *The Ancient Wisdom*, London, 1977.
Bates, Brian, *The Way of Wyrd*, London, 1983.
Benjamin, Harry, *Everyone's Guide to Theosophy*, London, 1969.
Bleakley, Alan, *Fruits of the Moon Tree*, London, 1984.
Bouteiller, M., *Chamanisme et Guérison Magique*, Paris, 1950.
Boyce, Mary, *Zoroastrians: Their Beliefs and Practices*, London, 1979.
Campbell, Joseph, *The Masks of God*, (4 vols.), London, 1973.
Castaneda, Carlos, *Teachings of Don Juan*, Harmondsworth, 1983.
——, *Journey to Ixtlan*, Harmondsworth, 1983.
David-Neel, Alexandra, *Magic and Mystery in Tibet* (Original title: *With Magicians and Mystics in Tibet*), London, 1932.
Davidson, H. R. Ellis, *Gods and Myths of Northern Europe*, Harmondsworth, 1977.
Deren, Maya, *Divine Horse: The Living Gods of Haiti*, London, 1953.
Dioszegi, V., *Problems in Mongolian Shamanism*, Acta Ethnographica, 1961.
——, article, *Encyclopedia Britannica*, fifteenth edition.
Dodds, E. R., *The Greeks and the Irrational*, Berkeley, 1951.
Easton, Stewart C., *Man and the World in the Light of Anthroposophy*, New York, 1975.
Eliade, Mircea, *Images and Symbols*, trans. P. Mairet, New York, 1969.
——, *Shamanism: Archaic Techniques of Ecstasy*, trans. W. R. Trask, Princeton, 1972.
Frazer, Sir J. G., *The Golden Bough*, abridged edition, Harmondsworth, 1978.
Gantz, Jeffrey (editor), *The Mabinogion*, Harmondsworth, 1976.
Gimbutas, Marija, *Gods and Goddesses of Old Europe*, London, 1974.
Graves, Robert, *The Greek Myths* (2 vols.), Harmondsworth, 1984.
Gray, Dr Leslie, interview in *The Yoga Journal*, July–August, 1984.

Guthrie, W. K. C., *The Greeks and Their Gods*, London, 1950.

Halevi, Z'ev ben Shimon, *The Work of the Kabbalist*, London, 1984.

Harner, Dr Michael, *The Way of the Shamans*, San Francisco, 1980.

Hatto, A. T., *Shamanism and Epic Poetry*, London, 1970.

Hultkrantz, Ake (with Backman, Louise), *Studies in Lapp Shamanism*, Stockholm, 1978.

——, *The North American Orpheus Tradition*, Stockholm, 1957.

Hummel, Siegbert, *Der Eurasiastische Traditionen in der tibetischen Bon Religion*, Budapest, 1959.

Jung, C. G. (and others), *Man and His Symbols*, London, 1964.

——, *Collected Works*, London, 1966.

Kerenyi, C., *Gods of the Greeks*, London, 1976.

Levi-Strauss, Claude, *Totemism*, trans. R. Needham, London, 1964.

Lewis, I. M., *Ecstatic Religion*, Harmondsworth, 1975.

Lommel, A., *Shamanism: The Beginning of Art*, New York and Toronto, 1970.

Lovelock, Dr James, *Gaia: A New Look at Life on Earth*, Oxford, 1979.

Markale, Jean, *Le Roi Arthur*, Paris, 1976.

——, *Women of the Celts*, London, 1975.

——, *Les Celtes et la Civilisation Celtique*, Paris, 1975.

——, *Le druidisme*, Paris, 1985.

Michelet, Jules, *Satanism and Witchcraft*, New York, 1946.

Muldoon, Sylvan and Carrington, Hereward, *Phenomena of Astral Projection*, London, 1951.

——, *Projection of the Astral Body*, London, 1931.

Needham, Joseph, *Science and Civilisation in China*, Cambridge, 1961.

Nelli, Rene, *Les Cathares*, Paris, 1972.

Onians, R. B., *Origins of European Thoughts about the Human Body*, Cambridge, 1951.

Radice, Betty (editor), *Hindu Myths*, Harmondsworth, 1975.

Rasmussen, Knud, *Intellectual Culture of the Iglulik Eskimo*, Copenhagen, 1929.

Rawson, P. and Lazslo, L., *Tao*, London, 1984.

Ross, Prof. Anne, *Pagan Celtic Britain*, London, 1974.

Rutherford, Ward, *The Druids*, Wellingborough, 1983.

——, *Pythagoras*, Wellingborough, 1984.

Schmidt, Father Wilhelm, *Origin and Growth of Religion*, trans. H. J. Rose, London, 1931.

Scholem, Gershom, *Kabbalah*, Jerusalem, 1977.

Sen, K. M., *Hinduism*, Harmondsworth, 1961.

Shirogokorov, S. M., *Psychomental Complex of the Tungus*, London, 1935.

Tzu, Lao, *Tao Te Ching*, trans. D. C. Lau, Harmondsworth, 1984.

Weber, Max, *The Religion of India*, trans. H. Gerth and D. Martindale, London, 1967.

Index

THE DRUIDS

Ward Rutherford
THE DRUIDS
Magicians of the West

The Doctrines, Beliefs and Practices of Druidism

Magicians of the West

Ward Rutherford. An illuminating and carefully researched study of the Druids, the mysterious pagan priesthood whose history is interwoven with fantasy, romance and folklore. A picture emerges of the Druids as guardians of the laws and social customs of Celtic civilization and the codifiers of the ideals upon which Celtic society was based. Describes the religious and magical practices of the Druids and their influence, through Merlin, on Arthurian legend.